Sauchiehall Street

Iain Heggie

T0262454

Methuen Drama

Published by Methuen Drama

1 3 5 7 9 10 8 6 4 2

First published in 2004 by
Methuen Publishing Limited

A CIP catalogue record for this book is available from the British Library

ISBN 0 413 77439 2

Typeset by Country Setting, Kingsdown, Kent

Vanishing Point presents

SAUCHIEHALL STREET

By Iain Heggie

Directed by Matthew Lenton

Designed by Kai Fischer

SAUCHIEHALL STREET

Sauchiehall Street was commissioned by Vanishing Point and opened at the Traverse Theatre, Edinburgh on 12 March 2004 with the following cast:

Dorothy	Jo Cameron Brown
Gerard	Peter Kelly
Maureen	Linda Duncan McLaughlin
Barry	Fraser C. Sivewright
Candice	Clare Yuille

Directed by	Matthew Lenton
Set/Lighting Designed by	Kai Fischer

Technical Manager	Sergey Jakovsky
Stage Manager	Lauren Brown
Deputy Stage Manager	Kerry Stirling

Production Photographer	Tim Nunn
Publicity Design	Greenlight Creative

Set built by	Stuart Nairn

Project Manager	Severine Wyper

Sauchiehall Street was developed with the help of the following students from the Royal Scottish Academy of Music and Drama:

Gordon Brandie, Joanne Cummins, Bryony Harding, Kirsten Hazel-Smith, Emun Mohammadi, Ionia Ní Chróinín, Allan Sawers and Rebecca Sloyan.

The production runs approximately 2 hours.
There is a fifteen-minute interval.

BIOGRAPHIES

Jo Cameron Brown (Dorothy)
Theatre: Regional Credits at Leicester, York, Chester, Manchester, Coventry, Watford, Pitlochry, Glasgow Citizens, Dundee Rep, Edinburgh Lyceum, including *A Midsummer Night's Dream, Cyrano, Woyzeck, The Boyfriend, Stepping Out, Cabaret, Hamlet, Guys and Dolls, Ride Down Mount Morgan, Slab Boys, The White Bird Passes, Macbeth* and *American Bagpipes*. Tours include: *Men Should Weep* (7:84); *The Guid Sisters* (Tron); *The Steamie* (Best Actress Nomination); *Sacred Hearts* (Communicado); *Sir Martin Mar-All* and Liz Lochhead's *Medea* (Theatre Babel). West End London: *Perfect Days, The Hang of the Gaol, Evita* (original cast) *The Beggar's Opera, Guys and Dolls* and *Square Rounds* (R.N.T). Television includes: *Cloud Howe, The Singing Detective, Sometime in August, Casualty, Great Expectations* and *River City* (all BBC); *Psychos, Brookside* (CH4); *Big Battalions; The Bill; Coronation Street; The Personal Touch; Cats Eyes* and *Inspector Lynley Mysteries*. Films: *Britannia Hospital, Pirates of Penzance* and *Bollywood Queen*.

Lauren Brown (Stage Manager)
Lauren graduated from the RSAMD with a BA in Technical & Production Arts. Design includes *The Man With The Flower In His Mouth* (visiting artist RSAMD). She has worked as a scenic artist on *Blindsight* (Untitled Projects/Tramway) and *The Slab Boys Trilogy* (Traverse Theatre Company). Lauren has also worked as a technician on *Living Cities* (Working Party) and as an assistant prop maker on *The Marriage of Figaro* (for RSAMD).

Kai Fischer (*Designer*)
Kai studied Audio-Visual Media at the HDM in Stuttgart. For Vanishing Point he recently co-directed and co-

designed *Stars Beneath the Sea*, *Invisible Man* and *A Brief History of Time*. Earlier work for the company includes the set and lighting designs for *Glimpse, Blackout* and *Last Stand*. Outside Vanishing Point Kai works as a freelance lighting designer. He has lit productions for many Scottish companies including 7:84, Citizens Theatre, Dundee Rep, Glasgow-Nuremberg Dance Alliance, KtC, Royal Lyceum Edinburgh, SweetScar, TAG, Theatre Babel and Tron Theatre Glasgow. With his work he has toured to Canada, France, Germany, India, Taiwan and the USA. As assistant lighting designer Kai recently worked on *Rheingold* and *Walküre* for Scottish Opera's *Ring Cycle.*

Iain Heggie (Writer)
Plays include *Politics in the Park, A Wholly Healthy Glasgow, American Bagpipes, The Sex Comedies, An Experienced Woman Gives Advice, The Don, The King of Scotland, Wiping My Mother's Arse* and *Love Freaks*. Radio plays include *Funeral Catering in the 21st Century* and *Zeitgeist Man*.

Sergey Jakovsky (*Technical Manager*)
Sergey graduated with a BA in Technical and Production Arts from the Royal Scottish Academy of Music and Drama in 2002, and is now developing his career of theatrical lighting and technical skills. Recent projects as Production/Technical Manager include *Living Cities Event* (Tory Glen), *Stars Beneath the Sea* (Vanishing Point), *A Brief History of Time* (Vanishing Point), *Word for Word* (Magnetic North). As Lighting Designer: *The Crysalids* (Tron Theatre), *Rescuers Speaking* (Birds of Paradise), *Emerge* (Architecture Exhibition), *Sharmanka Kinetic Theatre Installation* (Theatre Museum, London) *The Dawn* (Nomad) and *Soul Pilots* (ek performance). Other work includes interior lighting design for Bar Gandolfi in Glasgow and lighting technician for *Without A Trace* (Sounds of Progress).

Peter Kelly (Gerard)
Theatre includes seasons with the RSC (Stratford,
London and NewYork), Shared Experience (Japan, Korea,
Israel and UK tours), Citizens Theatre Glasgow and
Birmingham Rep. In London he has appeared in
MasterClass and *Brothers Karamazov* (also Edinburgh
Festival, Moscow, Lenningrad). At the Traverse Theatre
Edinburgh he has played leading roles in *The Hardman*
and *Walter.* TV work includes *A Touch of Frost, The
Bill, Taggart, Eastenders, The Amazing Miss Stella
Estelle.* Film includes *Welcome to Sarajevo, Surviving
Picasso, The Tall Guy* and *The Virgin Soldiers.* Recent
theatre work includes *If Only, The Prime of Miss Jean
Brodie* (Royal Lyceum Theatre), *Variety* (Grid
Iron/Edinburgh International Festival) and *Without A
Trace* (Tron/Traverse).

Matthew Lenton (*Artistic Director*)
Matthew is the founder of Vanishing Point and has
directed or co-directed all of the company's
productions. He has worked with the company across the
UK and internationally as director, writer and
performer. Outside Vanishing Point, Matthew has
directed for the Tron Theatre in Glasgow, the Traverse
in Edinburgh and the Royal Scottish Academy of Music
and Drama, where shows include *The Visit, The
Alchemist, The Mighty* and *The Three lives of Lucie
Cabrol.* As a writer he has been commissioned by LookOut
Theatre Company.

Linda Duncan McLaughlin (Maureen)
Linda trained at Guildford. Theatre credits include
Word for Word (Magnetic North), *Antigone, Julius Caesar*
and *Lanark* (TAG), *The Steamie* (Oldham Coliseum), *Piaf*
(Dundee Rep), *Men Should Weep* (Citizens) and *Jive!
Jive! Jive!* (Take Two) but she has played all over the
UK from the Orkney Islands to Plymouth. Film and TV

includes *Taggart* (STV), *The Key, Still Game, Monarch of the Glen, Murder Rooms, Bumping The Odds* and *Cardiac Arrest* (all BBC), *Bodyshifters* and *Alive and Kicking* (C4) and she can be seen in the upcoming *Solid Air* (Momentum Films). This is her first show with Vanishing Point.

Fraser C. Sivewright (Barry)
Fraser graduated from QMUC School of Drama in 2003 with a BA in Acting. At QMUC he performed in *Tartuffe, Marat/Sade, A Midsummer Nights Dream, Woyzeck, Twelve Angry Men, Victoria* and *The Suicide.* Professional theatre credits include *The Collected Works of Billy The Kid* (Fringe 2001) and *The Apprentice* and *It's A Wonderful Life* (Nonsense Room Productions). TV includes *Witchcraze* (BBC). Film includes *16 years of Alcohol* (16 Years), *The Host* (Simple Films) and *Once upon a Time* (Apollo Films).

Kerry Stirling *(Deputy Stage Manager)*
Kerry is currently studying Technical and Production Arts at the RSAMD, where she is specialising in Stage Management. Professional work outside RSAMD includes Assistant Lighting Designer on *The Dawn* (Nomad/Arches) and scenic artist on *Blindsight* (Tramway/Untitled). Kerry is on placement with Vanishing Point.

Severine Wyper (Project Manager)
Since graduating from Duncan of Jordanstone Art College in 1999, Severine has pursued an arts managerial role in various sectors. Her work to date has involved the development and management of art installation projects, multimedia projects and commercial websites. Since joining Vanishing Point, Severine has overseen projects such as *A Brief History of Time*, the international performances of *Invisible Man*, and the UK tour of *Stars Beneath the Sea*.

Clare Yuille *(Candice)*

Clare graduated from the RSAMD in July 2003. Since leaving college she has worked on radio drama for BBC Radio 4 and for the BBC Talent project. She appeared at the Royal Lyceum as Sandy in *The Prime of Miss Jean Brodie* while still at college and again more recently as Princess Irene in *The Princess and the Goblin*.

VANISHING POINT

Vanishing Point is a Glasgow-based company that tours inventive, ambitious new theatre to audiences across the UK and internationally. The company was founded in 1999 when its adaptation of Maurice Maeterlink's *Les Aveugles* set imaginations alight at BAC London and the Edinburgh Festival.

The company enjoys a strong reputation for atmospheric, exciting and evocative theatre that combines an often physical performance style with inventive design and collaborative development processes. The company collaborates with writers, visual artists, designers and other practitioners and is constantly exploring new methods of working.

Recent work includes:

Invisible Man

Invisible Man toured in the UK and to Ajaccio, Corsica and Festival Oest Nord Ouest, Theatre de Cornouaille, Brittany. *Invisible Man* is the wordless story of an improbable imposture. A violin maker and her husband make beautiful instruments for a brutal buyer, who profits by exporting them across the border to the city that glows in the distance. Hypnotised by dreams of the city and the freedom it offers, one night the man makes a break for it, leaving the woman to face the music. But nearby, a prisoner escapes from his cell and arrives at the house of the woman. Frightened at first, they soon begin a daring façade in the face of increasingly suspicious authorities. Combining physical performance, puppetry, projected digital imagery and an original music score, Invisible Man is a haunting and deeply atmospheric show.

A Brief History of Time

Based on Stephen Hawking's best selling book, *A Brief History of Time* is about the universe, time and the urge to explore that leads humankind on a potentially infinite search for knowledge and ultimate answers. Embarking in groups of twelve, audiences begin a visceral journey around the spaces of Tramway. They encounter performance, animation and a sound and video installation, before indulging in a sinister game of cards, which separates winners from losers. Winners are led one by one into the vast pitch darkness of Tramway 1, where faint images emerge from the darkness, before being led blindfolded into a nearby church. Here they are reunited with the losers, who have been on a journey of their own, for the final sequence.

Upcoming work includes

Lost Ones. A highly visual new show inspired by the work of Edward Gorey. A co-production with The Lemon Tree in Aberdeen, touring Scotland and the UK in October and November 2004.

ManCub. A collaboration with Douglas Maxwell in co-production with The Soho Theatre, London. Touring the UK in Spring 2005.

For Vanishing Point

Artistic Director	Matthew Lenton
General Manager	Severine Wyper
Artistic Associate	Kai Fischer
Technical Manager	Sergey Jakovsky
Marketing Associates	Rabbit PR
Board of Directors	Emily Ballard
	Greg Giesekam
	Nicola McCartney
	Audrey McIntosh
	Christine Walsh

Vanishing Point is registered as a
Scottish Charity, No. SC 028765

Vanishing Point, CCA, 350 Sauchiehall Street,
Glasgow G2 3JD   Tel. 0141 353 1315

www.vanishing-point.org

DIRECTOR S NOTES

A few people have asked me why Vanishing Point decided to do a play by Iain Heggie. One or two have said, 'it's not very Vanishing Point'. But what Vanishing Point likes is adventures. When I saw my first Heggie play I knew ˜something special was happening in the theatre. The audience were almost fighting each other. Young people, old ladies with blue hair, arty types with goatee beards. I loved the play. It was complex and funny, and touching but never sentimental. Here was a writer I wanted to work with. I wrote Iain a letter, care of the Traverse Theatre, where his *play Wiping My Mothers Arse* has just premiered, and the adventure began. Now, after a year working together, we have a story to tell. Iain has written the story. It is my job to make it work onstage and to take the audience on the adventure.

Matthew Lenton
Director

Vanishing Point is supported by The Scottish Arts Council and Glasgow City Council:

Thanks to:
Emily Ballard, Paul Iles, Greg Giesekam, Audrey McIntosh, Nicola McCartney, Simon Sharkey, Charles Bell, Jaine Lumsden, Nina Kirk, Hugh Hodgart, John Kazek, Lewis Howden and the second year acting students at RSAMD.

Sauchiehall Street

Characters

Dorothy Darvel, *actors' agent, sixties*
Gerard Galston, *Dorothy's husband, actor, sixties*
Candice Kilmaurs, *actress, twenties*
Barry Barr, *actor, twenties*
Maureen Mauchline, *trainee agent, forties*

Notes on the Text

. . . indicates a short break
/ indicates an interruption or interrupted train of thought

The playscript that follows was correct at the time of going
to press, but may have changed during rehearsal.

Scene One

An old Glasgow tenement room, reincarnated as an office. A window, two desks, one bigger and more in use than the other. A fax machine with a fax waiting to be read. A couch. Two entrances: one to flat, one to close and street. From blackout we hear a local radio station.

Gerard, in robe, comes in from flat, with breakfast. He goes to the smaller desk. He pushes desk items away carelessly so that they land on the floor. He settles to eat, nonchalantly. There is still not enough room. He goes to push the computer off the table and thinks better of it. He gets up and takes his breakfast to the other table. He pushes desk items to one side and settles to eat. Dorothy comes in from flat. Gerard doesn't look up. Dorothy puts radio off. Gerard looks up and they briefly catch each other's eyes and look away. She picks the boxes off the floor and arranges them on the smaller desk.

Dorothy What's wrong with the kitchen, dear?

Gerard You're always rushing in and out, talking shite.

Dorothy . . . Your bedroom, then?

Gerard Sad and lonely wank-filled place, with only me.

Dorothy . . . Well you could go to the living room surely?

Gerard Och no. TV sitting staring at you.

Dorothy Turn it off.

Gerard End up turning it back on. See if all the crap actors acting in their crap soaps or doing crap interviews on crap chat shows about *being* a crap actor *in* a crap soap are still as crap as ever. And you know what? They're even *crapper*. Not just chuck the TV out?

Dorothy You know perfectly well a TV is a necessity in my line of /

Gerard Well, give work up then. Slaving away at your age. It's obscene.

Dorothy I live for my work.

Gerard That's ridiculous. Living for your work. Could you not think of something more worthwhile to live for?

Dorothy   Such as?

Gerard   Such as me.

Dorothy   . . . You used to live for your work too!

Gerard   Been no point in living for you.

Dorothy   One of us had to make sure the bills were paid.

Gerard   While I was flouncing about being an ac-tor?

Dorothy   I was only too happy to . . . You know I . . . Your passion for acting used to burn like a . . . bright pure flame. What happened to it?

Gerard   It's all still burning away in here, on the quiet.

Dorothy   Could you not get it to speak up a bit?

Gerard   Och, what's the point? Nobody's listening.

Dorothy   No time for your cantankerous nonsense this morning. New start coming. (*Trying to usher him out.*) So if you could /

Gerard   She never seen a grown man stuffing his face before?

Dorothy   Quite a sheltered wee upbringing, the girl. First job.

Gerard   You always go for these school-leavers you can bully.

Dorothy   She is actually forty, dear.

Gerard   Mistake! Mature woman's hardly likely to let you torment the life out of her!

Dorothy   I beg your pardon. I don't torment my assistants. I confront them with the reality of the demanding profession they're entering.

Gerard   So what's the change of age for?

Dorothy   I'm looking for someone to take over the business.

Gerard Well, hallelujah! Excellent! But you never told me you were retiring. What's brought this on?

Dorothy I'm not retiring! Not yet. I'm just preparing for a . . . possible eventual retirement. It'll take several years — should she be suitable — to bring her up to the required standard. And I'll want a good price for my list.

Gerard The girl's got money then, I take it?

Dorothy No, but her mother's not getting any younger.

Gerard But you'll be stuck playing a waiting game till the old bird snuffs it. Can you not just give your list away as an act of charity? Stand you in good stead with the big man upstairs. (*Pointing up towards God.*)

Dorothy I've been up a close at the wrong end of Sauchiehall Street for thirty years, Gerard Galston. I'm not just going to let my work disappear into oblivion.

Gerard You'll die Dorothy Darvel. You'll die one day soon and your flesh will rot.

Dorothy What are you saying that for? Of course I'll . . . die. One day. That's why I'm leaving my mark on the world. Which is entirely natural.

Gerard Well, not one mark will I be leaving. Not one. And guess what? I couldn't give a —

Dorothy But you've given hundreds of wonderful performances that will live on in the memories of many.

Gerard Yes, and what happens when this 'many' dies? Their memories will die with them.

Dorothy . . . Be in a better mood if you got work.

Gerard I'm old and done. Nobody wants me.

Dorothy Och! You used to say there's parts for all ages in acting. It's just you. You've given up trying. Don't even do your voice exercises these days. You're away into a decline from the lack of occupation. Could you not put your old age to good use and / and / and . . . ?

Gerard   And what?

Dorothy   Do the same as me. Give something back to the world. Pass on your skills to posterity.

Gerard   Eh?

Dorothy   Become a mentor to a young actor.

Gerard   They're none of them interested in acting. It's all fame nowadays.

Dorothy   Yes, but under your tutelage! Because I know you'd be good. Crotchety but good. I can just picture you putting your finger on their wee problems.

Gerard   Aye you'd give and give and give to the young cunt. Soon as he's got what he wants it'll be offski. Exactly as I would have done. No, no. I'm an actor or nothing. Selfish through and through.

Dorothy   Well, get acting then.

Gerard   Well, get on the phone and get me a job then.

Dorothy   If only it was that easy. No one will work with you.

Gerard   I'm a gentleman in rehearsal.

Dorothy   You undermine the young directors.

Gerard   I'm giving them the benefit of my experience.

Dorothy   You tell them they 'know nothing about stagecraft and the art of voice'.

Gerard   Well, someone has to.

Dorothy   Yes, but not in front of the entire company.

Gerard   I'm an artist, not a spin doctor. And there's no work in Scotland I want. We're a small wet remote philistine country with a tiny population. A bunch of educationally subnormal idiots in nappies directing our plays. The dross no one else wants. I should've signed up with the RSC when I had the chance.

Dorothy   I had a business to build.

Gerard   You could have moved your 'business' to Soho.

Dorothy   Och London's no place to bring up a family.

Gerard   What family's that, Dorothy? Eh? What family's that?

Dorothy   . . . The RSC might have wanted you twenty-odd years ago. Scotland will have to do now.

Gerard   I've accepted my fate. A sad old loser who'll never work again or be remembered after his death. It's you that /

Dorothy   You know perfectly well you could find work if you'd just stop being so fussy, start behaving yourself in rehearsal and – once and for all – give up /

Gerard   Go on. Deny me my only pleasure.

Dorothy   I wouldn't mind. But two sessions a day, seven days a week! I mean: what time did you crawl home last night?

Gerard   Difference does it make? Back to an empty bed. It's like my tomb. Who cares whether I come back at all?

Dorothy   We may not be sleeping together. But it doesn't mean I take no interest in your welfare.

Gerard   Well, if I was late, no wonder. Cashpoint wouldn't cough up.

Dorothy   Oh?

Gerard   I'd to run after Duncan Devlin and make a tit of myself tapping him for my taxi fare. Any idea why?

Dorothy   Talk about it later, dear.

Gerard   'Talk about it later, dear.' Is there something I should know?

Dorothy   Please, dear.

Gerard   What's going on?

Dorothy Well that's you out of work two years now. And you know what you've been like.

Gerard What's going on, I said?

Dorothy Withdrawing like there's no tomorrow, but never ever paying in!

Gerard Dorothy, what's going on!

Dorothy I've transferred the remaining balance, dear.

Gerard Oh you have.

Dorothy Yes. I have.

Gerard And are you planning on giving me a card?

Dorothy Well it's not actually a joint account I've opened.

Gerard So I have to come to you for money?

Dorothy Only till you get yourself sorted out.

Gerard I am not going to play someone's grandad in a soap opera.

Dorothy Who said anything about soap opera? . . . Look, there's a nice film in . . . (*She takes out the fax.*) 'A general casting for all ages. Ewan Carlyle, starring, producing and directing.'

Gerard Not in a million years.

Dorothy Lovely man seemingly.

Gerard Take one. Cut. Take two. Cut. Cut. Cut. Cut. What do you call that? Where's the passion there?

Dorothy Can you not just take a wee holiday from passion and be professional for once? It brings in the cheques. Screen is the one medium where the work of the actor lives on.

Gerard For the last time, it's not me that minds disappearing into oblivion. If I had my way this bloody agency would go up in smoke and you'd take me on a / on a / on a /

Dorothy   On a what, dear?

Gerard   Well, if you must know: on a world cruise. Yes you heard me. On a big fat fuck-off world cruise to reacquaint myself with the woman I married. How is my wife these days, by the way? Good thirty years since I last saw her.

Dorothy   Och you. Run a mile if I offered to travel a couple of stops on a bus with you. We'll talk about world cruises just as soon as I can get the girl trained up to take over. So please just go, before she /

Maureen *comes in from street, dowdy.*

Dorothy   Oh, nice and early I see, Maureen.

Maureen   Oh, is it all right?

Dorothy   Yes an actors' agent is always punctual. This is Gerard.

Gerard   Hello Maureen.

Maureen   Oh, hello . . . Gerard.

He goes without breakfast things to flat.

Dorothy   Well have a seat.

Maureen *(jolted)*   Eh. Oh right . . . Where do you want me to . . .?

Dorothy   Now don't be nervous. An actors' agent is never nervous. Just pick one and sit on it.

Maureen *sits on the edge of the couch.*

Dorothy   Well, first things first. Your appearance.

Maureen   Oh, what's wrong with my −?

Dorothy   What did I say at the interview?

Maureen   Eh . . . you said /Well, you said / You said /

Dorothy   I said an actors' agent has to earn her respect. So smart dear, please. Smart at all times. An actors' agent is always smart.

Maureen   Oh do you not like what I'm wearing?

Dorothy   No I do not. It's dated and dowdy.

Maureen   Oh ah sorry Dorothy, I will try harder to /

Dorothy (*ominously*)   And as for your hair!

Maureen   What's wrong with my hair?

Dorothy   It's apologising for you. And an actors' agent never apologises.

Maureen   Even if they're in the wrong?

Dorothy   Particularly if they're in the wrong.

Maureen   Sorry.

Dorothy   Well, I'm not expecting you to know everything. Luckily for you. Because after all there's no point in your Aunty Dorothy shelling out a fortune in rates for an address in Sauchiehall Street only for you to lower the tone with inappropriate coiffure. And they've a cheek, quite frankly, the council. Because Sauchiehall Street's not what it was. In my day it was all department stores with educated assistants, tea rooms with chandeliers and a wide array of French patisseries. What is it now, I ask you? Gaudy lap-dancing bars, half-baked pedestrianisation schemes with cracked paving, polystyrene pizza-packaging by the skipload and rows of so-called fashion emporiums with outsize windows. Now did your mother get settled into her nursing home all right?

Maureen   Oh not bad. Fine, you know?

Dorothy   Tell your Aunty Dorothy the truth.

Maureen   Well, eh, she was actually screaming, swearing and kicking.

Dorothy   Oh, no need for that nonsense. We should all grow old gracefully. And serve the old bag right. Keeping you at home all these years, when you should be out working and getting a man like the grown woman you are.

Maureen   But there was no one else.

Dorothy Conniving old cow, that mother of yours. Not a thing wrong with her. What was her story again?

Maureen She lost both her legs in a car accident.

Dorothy You see. Do anything for attention, some of them. But good on you. You dumped the old cow in a home and settled her hash. But I can't stand here singing your praises all day long. Because an actors' agent is a hard worker. Now: / Oh would you look at that!

Dorothy *points to* **Gerard**'s *dishes.*

Yes, you see: an actors' agency is a business environment. Not a food establishment.

Maureen Oh but it wasn't me. I've only just /

Dorothy *snatches up dishes and goes out to flat, leaving* **Maureen** *at a loss for a few seconds, not knowing what to do. Phone rings.*

Maureen Aaaah!

Maureen *calms herself, then hesitates to answer.*

Dorothy (*off*) Well, answer it, dear. It might be the Glasgow Citizens' or the Royal Lyceum.

Maureen *picks it up.*

Dorothy (*head back round door*) And if it's a London agent telling me she's taken one of my clients tell her to / No, don't. Just put the phone down on the bitch.

Maureen (*confused, caught between answering and thinking she has to put the phone down*) Eh . . .

Dorothy (*off*) Answer the phone, Maureen.

Maureen Oh, ah, right, Dorothy. Right you are. (*To phone.*) Hello.

Dorothy (*off*) Dorothy Darvel. Theatrical Agency.

Maureen Eh . . . Dorothy . . . Darvel . . . Theatrical . . . Agency! . . . Oh, right. You want to see Candice Kilmaurs for (*Finding pen and writing.*) Lady MacDuff . . . And anyone

suitable for the part of Malcolm . . . and the part of King
Duncan . . . The Wee Theatre at . . . Alloa . . . Oh I'm
sure she's available . . . I'll check with Dorothy and . . .

Dorothy *comes in from flat.*

Maureen (*seeing* **Dorothy**)   That was the Wee Theatre at
eh . . .

Dorothy   Yes I heard you, dear. And quite frankly that
was – well I won't say it – because I'm not one to undermine
confidence. But do remember: hard to get, please. Hard to
get if you're an actors' agent. It's never ever 'I'm sure
they're available.' It's always always always 'I'll check their
availability and get back to you.' Now this Candice Kilmaurs.
Lovely actress. A college gold-medallist and a talent to be
reckoned with, there's no doubt about it. But far too big for
her boots. In here every day for the last two weeks checking
if there's any work. Wouldn't mind but after all the phone
has been invented. Doesn't seem to realise this is an agency,
not a green room. Yes, life in an actors' agency is an
education, is it not? I hope you're not too disappointed.

Maureen   Oh no. Not at all.

Dorothy   Tell your Aunty Dorothy the truth.

Maureen   Eh . . . em what about?

Dorothy   What did you expect to be doing all day?

Maureen   Eh . . . well I thought I would be helping
Shirley Maclaine and Robert De Niro with their careers.
You know, advising them on what the next step should be.

Dorothy   What country are we in, Maureen?

Maureen   Eh . . . well . . . Scotland would it be?

Dorothy   Exactly. So you'll have to content yourself with
the Robert McGonagalls and the Shirley Duffs of this world.

Maureen   I haven't actually heard of them.

Dorothy   Do you never watch television?

Maureen   Oh yes. But it was usually up to my mother what I got to see. And she used to say if it's not in black and white it'll leave a bad taste in the mouth, turn it off.

Dorothy   Well, your mother's off your back now, so it's about time the worm turned, isn't it?

Maureen   Oh absolutely. Very much so! . . . What worm's that, Dorothy?

Dorothy   . . . Now if you'll get on with the mail.

Dorothy *hands over the envelopes.* **Maureen** *takes them and hesitantly starts opening them.*

Oh no, dear. Oh no. Shred and bin. Shred and bin, please. Or we'll be here all day.

Maureen   Do you not want me to open them first?

Dorothy   Why would you want to do that? They're only actors CVs. (*Getting* **Maureen** *to feel the envelope.*) You see. Always tell by the photo.

Maureen   But have the actors not gone to a lot of trouble?

Dorothy   Oh yes. A lot of trouble they've gone to. Miles of trouble. Packing their CV with lies and paying a small fortune for a photographer to make them look nothing like they do in real life. The television and theatre companies aren't stupid. They know the difference between a glamorous young girl and a shipwrecked old crone. No, don't ever read actors' CVs. Not only would you die of boredom. Your truth-discerning faculties would suffer irreparable damage. On you go then!

Maureen *starts tearing up the envelopes. A bit nervously.*

Dorothy   I haven't got time for this. Put them down and get your coat.

Maureen   Oh you're not sacking me? I will get better. I promise.

Dorothy   Och nonsense girl. No heartless harridan me. New starts get plenty time to adjust to agenting. Plenty time.

Maureen, *bewildered, goes for her coat.* **Candice** *bursts in, with flowers, from street.*

Candice Hiya, Dorothy. Just passing. Thought I'd pop by. See how you are.

Dorothy Excellent, dear. Thank you. Just going out though.

Candice Och I won't keep you. You know me. This your new start? (*To* **Maureen**.) Maureen, isn't it?

Maureen Oh, hello.

Candice I'm Candice Kilmaurs. You'll love it here. Dorothy's fantastic. Best actors' agent in Scotland. And so respected. Totally honest. Treats her clients like human beings. Unlike all the other cunts. And you're gorgeous, by the way.

Maureen Oh, thank you.

Candice Smashing big knockers and everything. Gina Nardoni's heading south today, Dorothy. Seeing her off at the station. Stuff she's packed as well. I'm like, but you might not like London, Gina. You'll maybe want to come back if it doesn't work out. You should just take a couple of wee cases. It's only three per cent employment. And you're out three or four notes just for a coffee. Should totally of got Dorothy to take you on, that's what I said to her. ''D've kept her right about London, wouldn't you?' No telling her though. She's like, thanks for the encouragement. I'm like I'm just joking, Gina. Course it'll work out. Might be three per cent employment but as long as you're one of the three per cent that's well cool. It's just really me I'm thinking about, I said to Gina. Just because I'm not built for a massive huge city with hunners of famous people and millions to do and billions of money doesn't mean you're not. Just because I haven't the faintest idea who I am doesn't mean you don't know who you are. Any work in for me, by the way?

Dorothy I will call you. Soon as I've got something.

Maureen Oh Dorothy /

Dorothy (*signalling to* **Maureen** *to shoosh*) No need for you to keep calling by. Putting yourself to all that trouble.

Candice Aw, it's no trouble. I love coming here. Dead dead welcoming. And it's just that that's six months since I got out of college and I thought with me getting the gold medal and everything there'd maybe be something by now, you know?

Maureen But Dorothy / ?

Dorothy *signals* **Maureen** *to shoosh.*

Candice I mean: right now I'd take anything. Even a wee Gregory Greig or David Burke play would do. It's not as though I'm demanding a Shakespeare.

Maureen No but Dorothy, what about / ?

Dorothy (*signalling* **Maureen** *more emphatically*) Patience, dear. Patience is an essential for the long and arduous but not unrewarding actor's life.

Candice Och I know. It's just that my debts are mounting up and up and up. And my da's doing his nut because I've still not got a job.

Maureen (*to* **Dorothy**) But shouldn't you say something about / ?

Dorothy (*silencing* **Maureen**) Tell me about it on the way, dear.

Candice Nice meeting you, Maureen.

Maureen *nods.*

Candice (*to* **Dorothy**) Oh, and these are for you.

Candice *hands over the flowers to* **Dorothy**.

Dorothy Oh lovely, dear. Lovely. You shouldn't have.

Candice Bye, guys.

Candice *bounces out to street, jubilantly.*

Dorothy *dumps the flowers in the bin.*

Dorothy Cute these actresses. Trying to get round me with cheap supermarket flowers. Yes, you'll have to realise one very important thing, before you start butting in again . . .

Maureen What's that?

Dorothy Actors, dear, are all children . . . And I should know. I married one. But I'm able for them nowadays – oh yes – I stood up to that so-called husband of mine and said, 'So much and no more.' So be like me, Maureen, and give your actor the three S's. Shape, structure and strategy! You'll have them eating out your hand. That's why it's our duty as agents to screen the work that comes in and decide if they're ready. The Wee Theatre at Alloa is a lot of pressure on a young actress. It has an enviable reputation for production standards throughout the length and breadth of Clackmannanshire. And you have to be there for them, if they fall flat on their fanny. One critical panning could damage their confidence for many decades to come. You see now, Maureen?

Maureen I do, Dorothy. I do.

Dorothy And you don't want them getting ideas above their station. Half of them would be off down to London before they're ready. I've a notion that Gina Nardoni will be back within the week. A grand poorer – at least – and severely traumatised. And you've also yourself to think of. You knock your pan in for years on end to get their wee careers launched and then they think they can just up sticks and off to the golden pavements of London.

Maureen How could they do that to you?

Dorothy Easily, dear. All too easily.

Maureen I mean what could they see in London when they could stay here and get the three S's from you? I'd never go there.

Dorothy Exactly, dear. And you have to guage your actors with care. Because those that lack the essential attribute of guile would end up on the streets a pauper or a prostitute in that hellhole. And it would be your fault if they did. And you know the Wee Theatre at Alloa is only one of several offers I've had in for Candice Kilmaurs. One of many. And I'll decide which ones she gets to know about and which she doesn't. So encourage them to call round at Sauchiehall Street by appointment only. After all, we don't want our office cluttered with out-of-work actors, do we?

Maureen   Eh no.

Dorothy   And why is that?

Maureen   Eh eh is it because actors are all children?

Dorothy   It is, dear. It is.

She goes to go then turns back.

Dorothy (*ominously*)   Oh, and Maureen –

Maureen (*terrified*)   Yes?

Dorothy (*warm*)   Welcome to the glamorous world of show business.

Dorothy *breezes out to street.* **Maureen** *follows in her wake, looking at* **Dorothy** *in wonder, as if at a master.*

Blackout.

Scene Two

A few hours later. **Barry** *knocks tentatively and comes in. He looks round and goes to flat door.*

Barry (*shouting off*)   Hello! Anybody here?

Silence. He looks round and sits, tries to settle, tenses, realises he's tense, tries to relax, just beginning to when **Gerard** *comes in. Pause.*

Gerard   Typical. Bloody typical!

Barry (*standing*)   Eh . . . eh . . .

Gerard   Ever heard of ladies who lunch?

Barry   Eh . . . em . . .

Gerard   Well, she ain't no lady.

Gerard *goes to go laughing uproariously.* **Barry** *puzzling about something. Suddenly realises.*

Barry   I know you.

Gerard (*stopping in his tracks*)   I don't think so.

Barry   I do. I know who you are.

Gerard   I doubt it.

Barry   You're Gerard Galston. Aren't you?

Gerard *nods and goes to go.*

Barry   Well I saw your Macbeth and I thought you were great. Really amazing. Superb.

Gerard *stops in his tracks.*

Barry   See when you started killing all these wee guys I was like wow. I mean: I know all my mates from school were totally taking the piss. But I thought you were well cool. Gonny talk try and chat you up after the show. Then I thought, no. Guy'll think I'm totally at it because of all my mates pissing themselves laughing at him.

Gerard   . . . To which of my Macbeths are you referring?

Barry   You mean you've done it more than once?

Gerard   Many times. Many many times.

Gerard *goes to go.*

Barry   Well, it was at the Steeple Theatre. I was in my first year at secondary. Eight or nine years back must of been.

Gerard   Oh that one.

Barry   Not like it then?

Gerard   What was there to like? Director a prize wanker. (Aren't they all these days?) For reasons best known to

himself he set *Macbeth* in Nazi Germany with the witches
as drag queens in a Berlin night club.

Barry Yes but you reacted great when they started
whipping you with chains. Didn't know whether you loved
it or hated it. It was almost like kinky.

Gerard Shakespeare was not, as far as I'm aware, a sado-
masochist.

Barry Yes, but do you not think Shakespeare should be
updated for a contemporary audience?

Gerard Why would the audience need you to do that?

Barry So they can get all the contemporary parallels and
everything.

Gerard If contemporary parallels are so important, I'm
sure the audience can work them out for themselves. I think
you'll find it's just a case of egomaniac young directors
drawing attention to themselves.

Gerard *goes to go.*

Barry Well, do you not think you should be careful not to
sound like an old fart?

Gerard What if I am an old fart?

Barry Oh no. You're a great great actor. No way are you
a / It was seeing you made me realise what I wanted to be
when I grew up. Well? What do you say to that?

Gerard I say . . . how very gratifying. Goodbye.

Gerard *goes to go.*

Barry Well, I sent my CV in last week. Do you happen to
know if she got it all right?

Gerard Who?

Barry Dorothy.

Gerard No idea.

Barry That's why I called by actually. And to see if she maybe wanted to sign me up or anything.

Gerard Take my advice . . . try elsewhere.

Barry But she never got in touch. And people said she was probably just shooting the breeze when she said she would. And I'm getting sick sick sick of it.

Gerard Oh, it's all shooting the breeze, this business. It's all sick sick sick sickening. One sickener after another from the cradle to the grave. Get a proper job before it's too late.

Barry Can't believe someone like you would say that. Kind of thing my dad says. I mean: no way am I getting a proper job. I love acting. I want to play Macbeth at the Steeple Theatre and get whipped by drag queens.

Gerard Well get your diction and bearing sorted out.

Barry What's wrong with them?

Gerard They're a disgrace. You have the body of a wrecked ship and the voice of a dead pig, calling from the grave.

Barry Oh fuck.

Gerard What's the matter?

Barry You've totally gutted me. Am I really that bad?

Gerard You stoop, hobble, mumble and screech. You lack uplift, inspiration, charisma and technique. I mean: what do they teach you in the drama schools these days?

Barry Well improvisation and TV and radio and –

Gerard No voice, no movement?

Barry Never usually bothered going . . . Bar job at nights. Didn't make it in too often.

Gerard If you are an actor you'll work, or party, or fuck all night long and still make it in to class in the morning.

Barry Well hardly anybody else used to bother.

Gerard   Oh you want to be like everybody else, do you?

Barry   Well yes. Well no. It's you I want to be. I mean –

Gerard   What? This is ridiculous. You can't be me.

Barry   That's not what I meant. I meant I want to be *like* you.

Gerard   You can't even be like me. I'm forty years older than you. You have to be sensitive to the times you're living in and be an actor of and for your own generation. People would look at you like you're in a time warp if you tried to be me. All you can do is *learn* your skills from other artists.

Barry   Well, all right, I want to *learn* my skills from you. Or / or that guy Duncan Devlin maybe.

Gerard   Ugh. Used to be not bad. Sold out now. Television.

Barry   Well, what about Gordon Syme? He's excellent.

Gerard   Symey's a fool. A drunk. Come back tonight and you'll probably see him lying in the gutters of Sauchiehall Street.

Barry   So you don't drink?

Gerard   What kind of question is that? If you are an actor you must drink! Drink yourself into oblivion, wake up with the mother of all hangovers, face the void and all the other hellish facts of existence and haul yourself back up, look God in the eye and say: come on then, big man, I'm ready for you, I'll give you the Hamlet of the century.

Barry   Well, what about Ewan Carlyle? I wouldn't mind doing a wee bit of . . . learning from him. You must admit he's good.

Gerard   Well he's famous. I'll give you that. But good? I think not. He's the one that's always shooting his mouth off in the papers about how there's nothing to acting. A dawdle. Those that make it are privileged. The real heroes go out and slave in the shipyards. Well, I've got news for Ewan Carlyle: the art of acting is not a dawdle. Real actors live, eat and sleep the theatre. But then, of course, our Ewan has gone into the manky depths of the cinema. And am I sounding like an old fart again?

Barry   Oh no, you could never be an –

Gerard   I just happen to believe in the unique once-only occasion of that night, that audience, that performance. The magic of theatre, as someone once said!

Barry   Don't you like film acting then?

Gerard   What's there to like? It's just – what's the phrase? – saying the lines. Film is a form of pornography. Everything is *shown. Nothing* is left to the imagination. (*Goes to go.*) Now if you'll excuse –

Barry   Well, he said he thought I could be very good.

Gerard   Who did?

Barry   Ewan Carlyle.

Gerard   When?

Barry   He came to see our final-year show last year.

Gerard   Did he now? And what did you expect him to say? You were crap?

Barry   Well he said he'd give me the nod for a part in a film. If something comes up.

Gerard   And you think he will?

Barry   Took my number at least. Why? Think he won't?

Gerard *goes to go.*

Barry   Think Dorothy will want to sign me? It's just I'm getting all these radio ads. I need someone to sort out the paperwork and that.

Gerard *goes to go.*

Barry   Oh, and the guy's called Hamish Hunter. You heard of him? At all?

Gerard *shakes his head.*

Barry   Not do radio ads yourself, then?

Gerard *snorts.*

Barry   They're really good, though. Excellent money as well. And I can put you in touch with the guy. No, I can. Really and truly.

Barry *gives* **Gerard** *a card.* **Gerard** *goes to throw it away.*

Barry   And if you're embarrassed about doing ads that's OK, too. It's radio, remember. No one need know it's you.

This gives **Gerard** *pause for a second, then he bins it anyway.*

Barry   Aw, what did you do that for? The guy'd love you as well. It's not as if you stoop, hobble, mumble or screech or anything. So what do you reckon?

Gerard   Just in case you're in any doubt, I'm an actor, not a prostitute.

Gerard *goes to go.*

Barry   Oh Gerard.

Gerard   Yes?

Barry   I'm Barry Barr by the way.

Barry *offers his hand to be shaken.* **Gerard** *complies.*

Gerard   Pleased to meet you.

Barry   And I'm pleased to meet you.

Gerard *goes to go.*

Barry   Well could I possibly take you out to lunch sometime?

Gerard *stops in his tracks, gobsmacked.*

Barry   Thought you'd like to talk to me about my diction and bearing . . . You give me your time, I give you lunch. Seems fair enough. Yeah?

Gerard I don't think so.

Barry Oh, right. OK.

Gerard *goes to go.*

Barry No it's not OK. No way is it OK. Don't you realise what it took to put myself on the line like that? And you think you can just walk out. Just get up and walk out on me. And you're my top man as well. I'm well disillusioned now. Telling you, I don't start picking up a better vibe about my prospects I'm gonny give serious consideration to slashing my wrists. I can't believe I said that. That's just totally out of order. Because the only thing I'll be slashing's all this crap's that's totally getting in the way of me getting up where I belong. I mean I'm young and innocent and just starting out on life's journey. I deserve, need and demand encouragement.

Beat. **Gerard** *goes out to flat.*

Barry (*shouting after* **Gerard**) Aw, don't go, Gerard. Gerard! We haven't arranged a time for me to take you to lunch to discuss my diction and bearing. Come on. You know you want to. So what do you say? Gerard! Oh, fuck it. I'm coming after you.

Barry *follows* **Gerard** *to flat.* **Dorothy** *comes in, looks round, looks through flat door.* **Maureen** *comes in, made over, classically smart, from street.* **Dorothy** *turns back.*

Dorothy Well, don't say your Aunty Dorothy isn't good to you.

Maureen Oh I would never do that. Thank you very much!

Dorothy Och it's nothing. And always remember skimping is out of the question if you're an actors' agent. Because nothing succeeds like the appearance of success.

Maureen Don't say that. I mean, what if I don't succeed? Your investment will all have been for nothing.

Dorothy I beg your pardon. There was no investment on my part. Other than my time and expertise. No, dear. It's skimp and save if you're an actors' agent. So I'll be taking the price of your makeover out of your salary at the end of the month. Because an actors' agent is never a sponge. That's why I've had to take a tough line with my husband.

Maureen That's just like me.

Dorothy What's like you?

Maureen Well, my mother phones up the bank and tells them to give me ten pounds over the counter and not a penny more. And then she has the cheek to say, 'Cream buns, Maureen.' Cream buns and doughnuts and heart-rending cries. But I stand there on a daily basis and say, 'I can't afford cream buns on the budget you give me, mother.' No, I say, 'It's a raw carrot or do without.' Then I walk out while she pipes that in her smoke and shoves it. Ha ha ha. So I can be tough just like you, Dorothy, can't I?

Barry (*off*) Aw, Gerard! Let me in.

Dorothy *flicks a quick look at flat entrance.*

Maureen Can't I, Dorothy?

Dorothy Very good, dear. Excellent. Into actors' profiles now.

Maureen Eh . . .

Barry (*off*) Come on. Unlock the door, eh?

Maureen *looks up.* **Dorothy** *goes to flat exit and looks out.*

Dorothy (*bringing* **Maureen***'s attention back*) Actors' profiles, dear. And make a list of all available males in the nineteen-to-twenty-five bracket for the lovely part of Malcolm at the Wee Theatre in Alloa.

Maureen *starts work.* **Barry** *comes back in from flat.*

Barry That Gerard guy's playing hard to get with me taking him out to lunch. But he's wasting his time. I won't take no for an answer.

Dorothy   Who . . . are you?

Barry   Not remember me then?

Dorothy   Help me out, dear.

Barry   Aw! You chatted to me after my final-year show last year.

Dorothy   You all look the same to me, with your mass-produced fashions.

Barry   Well, you said I was to send you in my CV.

Dorothy   Yes, be in touch if we're interested.

Barry   You're giving me the brush off. Aren't you? I can tell! You can't do this to me. I'm very talented. I am. I've been told I am. By Ewan Carlyle, one of the greatest actors of his generation. Someone must want to represent me. I'm well gutted now. Telling you, I don't start picking up a better vibe about my prospects I'm gonny give serious consideration to slashing my wrists. I can't believe I said that. That's just well out of order. Because the only thing I'll be slashing's all this crap's that's totally getting in the way of me getting up where I belong. Have I said this before? Feeling I have. But so what? It needs to be said again. And again. Because I'm young and innocent and just starting out on life's journey. I deserve, need and demand a /

Dorothy   Do you know how to get to Buchanan Bus Station, dear?

Barry   I'm not giving you directions, you old sack of potatoes.

Dorothy   Second on the left, third on the right.

Barry   Find your own way, fat hips.

Dorothy   It's opposite the concert hall. You can't miss it. It was built in excessive haste for the year of culture and looks like the secret police headquarters in Warsaw. So be sure and not drift in there by mistake. Or you'll come out feeling you've been interrogated by Benjamin Britten or Ludwig van Beethoven.

Barry What are you going on about, you mad cow? And give me back my CV till I get out of this dump.

Dorothy I'm putting you up for the lovely part of Malcolm in the Wee Theatre's forthcoming production of *Macbeth*. (*To* **Maureen**.) Phone, dear.

Maureen *picks up the phone urgently, then hesitates.*

Barry Are you signing me up?

Dorothy I am, dear. I am. Because you are one of the most talented actors of your generation. People will be killing to get a ticket all over Clackmannanshire. And beyond. (*To* **Maureen**.) And get on the bloody phone, will you? Tell the Wee the boy comes with a recommendation from the great and famous Ewan Carlyle.

Maureen *hesitates.*

Barry Wow. That's amazing. I can't believe it. Yippy-dee-doo-dah!

Dorothy Off you go and catch that bus if you want to be an actor. Because the bus to Alloa is like your Aunty Dorothy. A dying breed.

Barry (*chanting at the top of his voice*) Woo-hoo. Woo-hoo. Woo-hoo.

Barry *goes out to street.*

Maureen How could you tell he was talented?

Dorothy Were we in the same room? Did you not see his performance?

Maureen Eh . . . what performance was that? Was he not being real?

Dorothy Of course he wasn't being real. 'Met Ewan Carlyle'? Yes if met means Ewan asking where the toilet is and our Barry piping up, 'Second on the left, third on the right, Ewan.'

Maureen But who actually *is* this Ewan Carlyle?

Dorothy Only the greatest actor of his generation.

Maureen But why would Barry lie?

Dorothy Because actors are all fantasy merchants. And so they should be. If they're any good at all they'll lie through their teeth and believe every word of it. Now if you'll get that number.

Maureen Oh, right away.

Maureen *finds the number and goes to dial.*

Gerard *comes in from flat.*

Gerard This is ridiculous. I can't go on like this.

Dorothy Like what?

Gerard No bloody money.

Dorothy What could you possibly need money for?

Gerard I said I'd meet Duncan Devlin today and pay him back what I owe him.

Dorothy Or to get pished out of your brains with him more like. Surely he can wait for a taxi fare?

Gerard I don't just owe him for a taxi. He's paid four lunches in a row. And he helped me out last week on a 9–1 at Redcar.

Dorothy I've stated my case. Find something useful to do or it's no go.

Gerard Like what?

Dorothy Like get that boy sorted out with his acting.

Gerard It'll take more than a few tips from me to sort out his inadequacies.

Dorothy He's got a vast acreage of passion.

Gerard   What's passion without technique? You can't reach the audience.

Dorothy   What's technique without passion? The audience won't care.

Gerard   I'm warning you, Dorothy Darvel. This is going to be the end of me.

Gerard *goes to bin, takes out the card* **Barry** *gave him.*

Dorothy   What are you doing?

Gerard *looks at her and goes to go.*

Dorothy   Well where are you going?

Gerard *stops in his tracks without looking back. Then he goes to go.*

Dorothy   He needs all the help he can get, that boy. I've put him up for Malcolm at the Wee.

Gerard (*stopping in his tracks*)   Why wasn't I told about this?

Dorothy   We've only just sent him.

Gerard   I didn't mean him. I meant the Wee doing *Macbeth*.

Dorothy   According to you you've retired . . . Not interested are you?

Gerard   No of course not. With that prick Ralphie Houston running the place?

Dorothy   Och dear, you're so out of touch. Ralphie got his jotters months ago for being pissed in rehearsal once too often. They've got a Jeremy Jennings up from Cambridge now. If you'd at least read the Sunday supplements you'd know his reputation as a wunderkind's gone ahead of him. Will I put you up for it?

Gerard   Seven weeks in Alloa? Better to die in the gas chambers.

Dorothy   Close your eyes, dear. Pretend it's Stratford on Avon.

Gerard   'If 'twere done when 'tis done then 'twere well 'twere done quickly.'

Dorothy   Is that a yes?

Gerard   What a part! What a part!

Dorothy   Well, seemingly the lead's gone. I was thinking maybe King Duncan.

Gerard   Oh don't be ridiculous. I'm far too young.

Dorothy   Don't look a day over fifty of course, but I'll remind you you are sixty-two.

Gerard   Sixty-one.

Dorothy   Yes, but remember the magic of theatre. You can be sixty-one looking fifty and playing ninety and the audience will believe it. Away through and talk to young Jeremy at least.

Gerard   Oh. Oh. Oh. Oh. Been so long. Don't know if I can cut it still. Acting's pure muscle. You have to keep it active.

Dorothy   Well, it's not exactly the RSC. It's only the Wee Theatre in Alloa. Are you forgetting it only seats thirty and no one ever goes?

Gerard   No no no no no no no no no no no no! And that's final. When does the job start?

Dorothy   Five weeks.

Gerard   Five weeks?

Dorothy   Yes.

Gerard   Five whole weeks, did you say?

Dorothy   Yes!

Gerard   That's ridiculous. I can't wait five weeks for money!

Gerard *goes out to street, with card.* **Maureen** *has found Alloa's number and is dialling.*

Dorothy   Gerard says yes too, dear.

Maureen (*nodding to* **Dorothy**, *then to phone*)   This is the Dorothy Darvel Theatrical Agency. One of the most talented actors of his generation – a Barry Barr – is on his way to see you. He comes highly recommended by the great and famous Ewan Carlyle for the lovely part of Malcolm. We can also offer you a Gerard Galston. Though looking sixty-one he is in actual fact ninety and can easily play fifty. That's the magic of theatre, you see. Both actors are for your forthcoming production of, eh . . . what is it again?

Dorothy *cringes*.

Blackout.

Scene Three

Several days later.

Gerard *found onstage.*

Gerard   Fiddle-dee-dee, fiddle-dee-da. Fiddle-dee-dee, fiddle-dee-da. Fiddle-dee-dee, fiddle-dee-da. Fiddle-dee-dee, fiddle-dee-da. Titty-ta-tee. Titty-ta-ta. Titty-ta-tee. Titty-ta-ta. Titty-ta-tee. Titty-ta – (*He stops his exercises abruptly and picks up the phone and dials.*) . . . Hamish Hunter? . . . Gerard Galston here . . . It was just about collecting my fee . . . Oh, OK, OK. I'll call back before the end of the week . . . Bye now. (*He puts the phone down. Under his breath.*) Fuck. (*Then, instantly snapping out of his annoyance.*) Bi-di-bi-baah. Bi-di-bi-boh. Bi-di-bi-baah. Bi-di-bi-boh. Mi-ni-mi-nah. Mi-ni-mi-noh. Mi-ni-mi-nah. Mi-ni-mi-noh.

Dorothy *comes in briskly and sees him. She coughs. He carries on She motions him to wind up.*

Gerard (*in her face*)   Mmmmmmaaah. Mmmmmmaaah.

Dorothy   All right, dear. Starting work now.

Gerard *stops*

Dorothy (*turning away*)   Thank you.

Gerard (*in her ear*)   P-B-P-B-P-B-P-B-P-B-P-B-P-B.

Dorothy   You're an evil man, Gerard Galston. Always have been. Always will be! Only happy when you're working!

Gerard (*dancing about*)   Fu-fu-fu-fu. Fu-fu-fu-fu. Fu-vu. Fu-vu. Fu-vu. Fu-vu. Fu-fu-fu –

Dorothy   And I'm at my wit's end sorting out that new start. Not conversant with the repertoire. Thinks Hamlet is a kind of cigar and Othello a cheap Italian wine. And my actors are deserting me in droves for the London vultures. Thirteen in the last year. And not so much as a postcard for their Aunty Dorothy from the West End. Even that talented basket case Candice Kilmaurs is under suspicion now. Four days. Four days and not a peep. If I can't stem the flow I might as well pack the whole thing up and go home.

Gerard   Meee-meee-meee-meeeeeh, meee-meee-meee-meeeh.

Dorothy (*shaking her head as she goes to go*)   Self-self-self when you're happy, self-self-self when you're unhappy. (*Stopping in her tracks.*) Oh, and don't be rude to the Cambridge wunderkind. Here.

*She takes out twenty pounds and gives it to **Gerard**.*

Gerard   Twenty pounds? What am I supposed to do with that?

Dorothy   Bus fares and lunch in Alloa. And count yourself lucky.

Gerard   But I haven't had a drink in four days.

Dorothy   Yes, and long may it continue. You're like a different person. There'll be more if you get the job.

Gerard   What about the mentoring money?

Dorothy   You haven't done any yet.

Gerard   But I will as soon as he puts in an appearance.

Dorothy   I thought you'd ruled it out.

Gerard Well, the theatre's given me so much over the years. I think it's about time I gave something back. Don't you? Li-ti-dee-da. Li-ti-dee-da. Li-ti-dee-da.

Dorothy *takes out another twenty-pound note.*

Gerard You'll get your reward in heaven.

Dorothy I wouldn't mind getting it here on earth.

Gerard Certainly. What would you like?

Dorothy I'd be quite happy for you to stay on the wagon.

Gerard Permanently?

Dorothy It would be like getting the old Gerard back.

Gerard (*faux smoochy*) And would Gerard get the old Dorothy back?

Dorothy We'll keep the bedroom situation under review, dear.

She hands over the other twenty-pound note.

Gerard (*breathing on* **Dorothy** *performatively*) Li-ti-di. Li-ti-di. Li-ti-di. Li-ti-di. Li-ti-di.

Dorothy *goes out, wary like a woman.*

Gerard Mmmmmaaaah. Mmmmmaaaah. Mmmmmaaaah.

Barry *comes in, watches for a few seconds, unsure whether to interrupt or not.*

Barry Hi, Gerard.

Gerard Mi-ni-mi-nah. Mi-ni-mi-noh.

Barry (*louder*) Gerard, hi!

Gerard Mi-ni-mi-nah. Mi-ni-mi-noh.

Barry Do that every day?

Gerard Mi-ni-mi / Every single day.

Barry Wish I'd your discipline. And listen, right? Still want me to get you lunch?

Gerard Not at all. Not . . . at . . . all. It's me that should be buying you lunch. And I will do. If we can find somewhere in darkest Alloa.

Barry Oh, do you know if I got the part?

Gerard More fool them if they don't. You're one of the most talented actors of your generation.

Barry Wow, man. Wow. I can't believe *the* Gerard Galston said that about me. But what about my diction and bearing?

Gerard Oh, what are diction and bearing beside raw passion? Which you have a vast acreage of.

Barry Aw, thanks very much. Thanks a . . . So you're going to Alloa too?

Gerard Assuming they have me.

Barry Why wouldn't they? You're the one and only Gerard Gal –

Gerard We'll rip Clackmannanshire in two, you and I. We'll rip it apart. Diddy-dee-dooh. Diddy-dee-dum. Titty-tee-tooh. Titty-tee-tum.

Gerard *goes out to street, tossing a mad smile at* **Maureen** *coming in with the mail, unseen to* **Barry**.

Barry (*larking about*) Oh wow, man. Wow. Titty-tee-tooh. Titty-tee-tum. Dibbly-doo. Dibbly-bum.

Maureen *coughs.*

Barry Lily-lolly-lally. Lily-lolly-lally. Billy-bolly-fluppetty-grunge. Billy-bolly-fluppetty /

Maureen Excuse me. Have you got an appointment?

Barry Well no. Just in to see if you'd heard. From Alloa. That's all.

Maureen Call you as soon as we do.

Barry Do you want me out?

Maureen   Don't want the office cluttered with out-of-work actors, do we? Creates a bad impression.

Barry   On who? Other out-of-work actors?

Maureen   I, eh / 1 eh / (*She rips up letters furiously.*)

Barry   What are you doing? You're not even opening them!

Maureen   We will ring you if anything comes up. The phone has been invented.

Barry   What?

Maureen   Well, that's what Dorothy always says. When an actor calls by without an /

Barry   Well, I'm sorry and all that. I mean: how was I to know what Dorothy says?

Maureen   And don't interrupt, dear. An actors' agent never interrupts!

Barry   What are you talking about? I'm an actor, not a −

Maureen   Oh that's right. So you are. Interrupt away then. Interrupt to your heart's content. Go on. Your Aunty Maureen says you can /

Barry   And what's with the Aunty Maureen? You're not my /

Maureen   Oh eh well what should I call you then? Because Dorothy always /

Barry   Call me what you like. But you're not my aunty, OK?

Maureen   Oh right! I'll not call myself your aunty. I'll call myself / eh / eh /

Maureen *resorts to ripping up the envelopes furiously and dumping them in the bin.*

Barry (*getting the letters back out*)   Look why are you doing that?

Maureen Actors' CVs are full of lies and expensive photographs that look nothing like they do in real life. I mean, the theatre and television people do know the difference between a glamorous old crone and a shipwrecked young girl, you know!

Barry That's ridiculous. Actors have gone to a lot of /
This is mine! That's my picture you've destroyed. That cost me hundreds of / And it does so look like me.

He holds up ripped bits of his photograph.

Maureen Well that's what Dorothy says.

Barry You know you'll need to get a grip. You're beginning to sound like Dorothy. (*Spookily.*) Or maybe you're even becoming Dorothy! (*He dumps his ripped photo in the bin.*)

Maureen Oh ha ha. Thanks very much. That's the nicest thing anyone ever said to me. She's the best in the business apparently. Treats her clients like cunts, you know. Unlike all the other human beings.

Barry What are you talking about? It's fine to be Dorothy if you're Dorothy. Apart from anything else, she's twenty years older than you. You have to be an . . . an . . . an actors' agent of and for your own generation. People'll look at you like you're in a time warp. Ha ha.

Maureen Who should I be like?

Barry Well, I don't know. Like you. Like someone from now. (*Scoffingly.*) I mean: I totally look up to Gerard and want to learn off him, but not to be him, for God's sake!

Fax erupts into life. **Maureen** *snaps out of it and goes to collect it.*

Maureen Well, congratulations, dear. Oh sorry for sounding like Dorothy there. You're not a dear at all. You're a / you're a / What are you?

Barry Never mind what I am. Why did you congratulate me?

Maureen Because / Because / Oh yes, because it says here, 'The Wee Theatre at Alloa were most impressed with your audition and are making you an offer.'

Barry Aw, they are not, are they? Are you serious?

Maureen (*nodding*) Of course they are. You're one of the most talented actors of your generation. Your passion is unprintable. Alloa. Ten for ten-thirty. A week on Monday.

Barry Aw wow, man. Wow. Thank you so much, Maureen. Thank you so much. This is the best day of my young life. Acting in my professional debut with my mate the great Gerard Galston. On an actual stage. At the world famous Wee Theatre in Alloa. In *Macbeth*. And now I'm going to lunch with Ewan Carlyle. Yippy-dee-doo-dah.

Beat, then **Maureen** *laughs suddenly.*

What is it? Why are you laughing?

Maureen Oh, you know: Ewan Carlyle.

Barry What's funny about that?

Maureen Well, you don't really know him, do you?

Barry Are you calling me a liar?

Maureen Oh no. Of course not. You know him really well. He's your best friend. Ha ha.

Barry Well, I wouldn't go that far. Not yet anyway. I mean: he lives in Los Angeles after all.

Maureen (*humouring him*) And are you going to have lunch with him in Los Angeles?

Barry No! He's back home in Glasgow to make a film. Sounds amazing. About the life of Saddam Hussein.

Maureen Who's . . . Saddo . . . Moosane?

Barry Oh only the most wanted man on the planet.

Maureen Oh is Saddo an actor too then?

Barry No! He got caught hiding down a hole in the middle of Iraq.

Maureen *laughs.*

Barry What are you laughing at now?

Maureen   Oh, just something Dorothy was saying about actors all being fantasy mantelpieces. So true. So true.

Barry   What?

Maureen (*humouring him*)   So tell me: has this Saddo Moosane ever been to Glasgow?

Barry   No, of course not. He's –

Maureen   So why are they filming his life story here?

Barry   Well . . . the architecture in the housing estates is identical to shagged-out slums of Baghdad. And all the old half-demolished shipyards make the Clyde an excellent stand-in for the Tigris-Euphrates seemingly. Dibbly-doo. Dibbly-bum. Dibbly-doo. Dibbly-bum. Titty-tee-tooh. Titty-tee-tum. Titty-tee-tooh. And ta-ta to you.

Barry *goes out to street jubilant, chanting, as* **Dorothy** *comes in from flat.*

Dorothy   Morning Maureen.

Maureen   Oh yes. Morning. Dorothy.

Dorothy   Now please tell me you did hear from Candice before you left last night?

Maureen   Oh no. Sorry. Nothing.

Dorothy   Four days now. That's four days now, dear.

Maureen   Maybe she's got the message she's an out-of-work office and she's not to be in cluttering up the /

Dorothy   You're too optimistic to be an actors' agent. Actors never get the message. Ring and see what's happened to her.

Maureen   Oh right away, Dorothy.

Maureen *looks in the computer for* **Candice**'s *number.*

Dorothy (*distractedly*)   And how's your mother today?

Maureen   Eh well she's actually shat the bed.

Dorothy Oh dear. Could you not find a more humane way of putting it? An actors' agent would never use that kind of language.

Maureen Is that a present-day actors' agent or one that's twenty years out of date, do you mean?

Dorothy What – exactly – are you trying to say?

Maureen Well the auxiliaries say shat the bed, and I don't want them to look at me like I'm from another era.

Dorothy The word is inappropriate for an actors' agent of any era. Say soiled and spare your poor mother's feelings. Oh listen to me. Talking as though your mother's my best friend. I'm far too soft to be an actors' agent. Always have been. Always will be.

Maureen Oh ho ho you're not soft, Dorothy. Look how you don't let out-of-work actors clutter up the /

Dorothy Oh you don't know your Aunty Dorothy. You don't know her at all, dear. She loves her actors like a mother, you see. So she just can't help indulging them. Not that any of them have ever shown any gratitude. Off to London the minute her back's turned, most of them. Yes it's a constant battle keeping them under lock and key. Now get on the bloody phone and get that Candice Kilmaurs round to Sauchiehall Street. Tell her she's up against a number of other actresses for the lovely part of Lady MacDuff.

Maureen But she's not up against other actresses. The Wee Theatre in Alloa have asked for her specially.

Dorothy Oh, split hairs why don't you? Don't you realise it's lie, lie, lie in the glamorous world of show business? It's lie, lie, lie till you're sick of lying. If you're to be an actors' agent. Oh. Oh. Oh. Oh.

Dorothy *rushes out to flat, crying.* **Maureen** *looks on in wonder, then picks up the phone and dials.*

Maureen (*to phone*) Good news, Candice, dear. Only I've not to say, dear. I've to say . . . Well, I don't know what

I've to say, but as soon as I find out I'll phone you back and tell you. And, eh, by the way you're up against a number of talentless nobodies for the lovely part of Lady MacDuff at the Wee Theatre in Alloa's forthcoming production of eh . . . eh. Well, just think yourself lucky it's Alloa. It's only a hellhole in the middle of nowhere. Because it could have been the RSC that asked for you. And they're away out in the slicks. And the London critics would have been giving your fanny a good panning. So come round to Sauchiehall Street to your . . . to your . . . Aunt Maureen soon as you get this. And just in case you haven't heard, Saddo Moosane's been found in a hole in the middle of a crack. Bye now, Candice. Bye.

Maureen *puts the phone down. She considers what she has said, then goes back to desperately tearing up envelopes.*

Blackout.

Scene Four

Next day. **Dorothy** *comes in, in robe, from flat. She goes out to street exit. She comes back in a few seconds later with mail and puts it on* **Maureen**'s *desk. She goes to phone and presses answering machine button.*

Machine Voice   You have no unplayed messages.

She slumps despairingly into her seat, puts her head in her hands and lets her hands fall to the desk. **Maureen** *comes in, in coat.*

Maureen   Oh Dorothy. What's wrong?

Dorothy *(perking up)*   Nothing wrong with me, dear. What's it to me if Candice Kilmaurs has disappeared off the face of the earth? She's just another actress.

Maureen   I'm sorry, Dorothy. I'm really / Do you think anything's happened to her?

Dorothy   Oh, positive attitude at all times, please. A positive attitude if you're to cope with the highs and lows of life as an actors' agent. The girl'll be walking out her flat to catch the bus to Sauchiehall Street as we speak. You mark my words. And how's your mother?

Maureen Well, I hardly saw her last night. Wet herself the moment I arrived. Then by the time the staff got her sorted visiting hour was over.

Dorothy Must be heartbreaking to realise she's even taken to sabotaging your wee visits with urine. You must be wondering if all these years of sacrificing your own life and not getting a man have been worth it. Well, I assure you they have. Marriage is not all it's cracked up to be. Two in the morning, dear. Two in the morning he staggers in. Not so much as a phone call. And straight to bed. Doesn't even have the decency to knock my door, wake me up and let me get a good night's sleep.

Maureen What do you think he was doing?

Dorothy Having his cock sucked by a young actress, what do you think he was doing? I mean, get real, dear. He's been in every second-rate actress's mouth in Scotland. And they're welcome to him. Slobbering all over them with his boozy breath and his beer farts. Then all his stories about how big he was in the seventies and how he never touches film. Yes, you have so much to learn about actors. First sniff of work and they're out drinking till all hours, bonding with the company and shagging for Scotland. Then soon as the work stops: under your feet all day long. Wallowing in their own misery. So take my advice and never trust an actor!

Maureen I won't, Dorothy.

Dorothy But when I think of all I've done for that husband of mine.

Maureen What have you done for him?

Dorothy (*suddenly sharp*) Run myself ragged keeping him from the truth's what I've done for him! (*Softening.*) Children, dear, you see. All children actors. Not one of them can face the harsh realities of life.

Maureen What did you keep from him?

Dorothy Never you mind being so nosey. You'll have all my secrets out of me if I'm not careful . . . Though I will say this: I'd to lie through my back teeth to keep him away from the RSC.

Maureen (*confidentially*) Is the RSC an actress then Dorothy?

Dorothy No it is not. It's just a vastly overrated over-funded theatre company. Every talentless nobody in Scotland thinks three months there as Third Servant in one of the *Henrys* will set them up for life.

Maureen So was it because of the actresses at the RSC you didn't want him to go there, Dorothy?

Dorothy Och dear. There's actresses throughout the globe. Keeping Gerard away from actresses would be like holding back the Atlantic. No, no the problem with the RSC is the London critics are misguided enough to attend it on a regular basis. And think what would have happened if they'd savaged Gerard? God alone knows a harsh word from the *Alloa and Clackmannanshire Gazette* would send him into a month's long drinking frenzy And don't you be mentioning any of this to my husband. Because an actors' agent never gives away secrets!

Maureen Oh I won't. I won't give away any of your secrets. I can assure you of that . . .

Dorothy Yes, miles better off single, dear. That's why you're perfect material to be an actors' agent. How long do you think your mother's got?

Maureen How long has she got till what, Dorothy?

Dorothy Till she / Till she / . . . Till she's better! What did you think I meant?

Maureen Well, the nurses keep shaking their heads and saying: 'Bear up, Maureen. She won't hold on much longer.' Do you think that means she'll be better soon?

Dorothy   Let's . . . hope so, dear. We can but hope. Funny not hearing from Candice, all the same. She could at least have had the decency to phone up and tell us a pack of lies.

Maureen   She's maybe not listened to my message yet.

Dorothy   Och, dear. If actors think there's a message from their agents on the go, they'd stop in mid-orgasm to listen . . . What exactly did you say to her?

Maureen   Just to pop round to Sauchiehall Street. The Wee Theatre in Alloa want to see her for the wonderful part of . . . of . . .

Dorothy   Oh no. Oh no, dear. Tell me you didn't mention Alloa.

Maureen   But I thought that's what you wanted.

Dorothy   Candice's cohorts will open their big mouths and tell her Alloa is a hellhole in the middle of nowhere and the Wee Theatre would sit like a blemish on the girl's CV for many years to come.

Maureen   But Alloa's not a hellhole. It's got a reputation throughout the length and breadth of Clackmankyshire.

Dorothy   You'll never make an actors' agent at this rate. Of course Alloa's a hellhole, dear. Of course it is. The worst known to mankind. Oh, listen to me. Just as well we're not in a play, or Clackmannanshire Council would be trying to get us banned. Now away round to Candice's and bring her back round to Sauchiehall Street. Then you can sit her down, look her straight in the eye and tell her Alloa has an increasing reputation as the Athens of the North.

Maureen *hesitates.*

Dorothy   Well, get her address first, dear.

Maureen   Oh right you are. Sorry.

Maureen *presses keys on computer and makes a note. She goes to go, then thinks better of it.*

Oh and could you possibly make up your mind whether I'm perfect material to be an actors' agent or not, Dorothy? It's just that one minute you think I am, the next minute /

Dorothy Oh, rub it in, why don't you? I'm far too emotional to be an actors' agent. Always have been, always will be. Unlike you, dear. No no I'm fully confident you will make the best actors' agent in Scotland and take over from me. If and when the time comes.

Maureen Oh do you want me to take over from you, Dorothy?

Dorothy (*outraged*) I can't believe you could actually say such a thing. I'll need to watch out for you. You'll have me dumped in my coffin before you can say the Wee Theatre at Alloa. (*Suddenly breaking into hilarity.*) Ha ha ha. Yes, you're an evil bitch after my own heart.

Maureen Oh, thank you, Dorothy. Thank you. Thank you. Thank you. Thank you.

Maureen *rushes out to street, beaming.* **Dorothy** *picks up the mail and starts ripping it up distractedly.* **Gerard** *strolls in from flat, in robe, with breakfast.*

Gerard (*into* **Dorothy***'s face*)
　　Thy crown does sear mine eye-balls. And thy hair,
　　Thou other gold-bound brow, is like the first.
　　A third is like the former. – Filthy hag,
　　Why do you show me this? (*Grabbing a ripped letter.*)

Dorothy I can't go on, dear.

Gerard What a play! What a play!

Dorothy I said I can't go on, dear.

Gerard Four-hundred-plus years old, it's never been bettered and I doubt it ever will. You were saying?

Dorothy Which slack-fannied actress was it this time?

Gerard Jeremy Jennings.

Dorothy Oh pull the other one.

Gerard   No, seriously. I take it all back. The boy's charming, clever, creative and, last but not least, he *knows how to talk to actors!*

Dorothy   So you got the job?

Gerard   Well he did ask me out for a drink.

Dorothy   Oh God. Oh God. Don't tell me.

Gerard   Why? What's wrong with investing a few pounds in my future employer.

Dorothy   It's not the money that's the problem. It's you opening your big drunken cakehole and yakking. Tell me the worst. What did you say?

Gerard   Och just light banter. Drollery. Prattle. You know the type of thing. Told him most of his ideas were terminally insane. That Alloa wasn't ready for the *Eskimo Macbeth*. That the actors would bake inside the oilskins and rebel on the grounds he was being a pretentious young cunt. Oh yes, and last but not least: 'What rhubarb, senna or what purgative drug, Would scour these English hence?'

Dorothy   Oh well done. First chance of work in months and you confine yourself to gratuitous insults. Sure you didn't manage to swing a few punches?

Gerard   He laughed his tiny Cambridge tits off! He laughed them clean off.

Dorothy *goes to flat, shaking her head.*

Gerard   Oh, Dorothy.

Dorothy *stops in her tracks.*

Gerard   Any chance of some money?

Dorothy   I gave you money yesterday. What have you done with it? Oh, don't answer that. Stupid question. You'll get more when the Alloa job's in the bag.

Gerard   Aw, Dorothy!

Dorothy   Not a moment sooner, dear. Not a moment sooner.

Dorothy *goes.* **Gerard** *slumps in front of his food. After a second he picks up the phone and dials.*

Gerard   . . . Hamish Hunter there, please? . . . When do you think he'll be back? . . . Gerard . . . Galston! Gerard Galston, tell him . . . He'll know what it's about . . . But do say it's getting urgent.

Gerard *puts phone down and goes back to food as* **Barry** *comes in.* **Barry** *goes up to* **Gerard** *and retreats, goes up and retreats, goes up, but* **Gerard** *ignores him, gets up and heads out to flat.*

Barry   Gerard. Gerard. Gerard, my man. Ewan Carlyle's actually offered me a part in his film and all my mates are sick sick sick sick sick sick! And its enough money to . . . to . . . to make all my mates sick-sick-sicker. But all I can think about is what you're gonny say . . . Well it's only a small part. I'll hardly be seen. Just an obscure nephew of Saddam's. Just carry out a couple of tortures and give the go-ahead for a few assassinations-type things. Ha ha. Well, it's not definite. It's just an audition. The producers have to see me first. And my heart will always be in the theatre!

Gerard   Ever seen what film actors do when they get back to the stage? Their so-called first love. Can't project, don't know how to move, don't know how to stand, no presence. It's all too mini. But what does that matter? The public will still turn up in their thousands to catch a glimpse of your shrivelled genitalia. And you know what happens to small parts in films, don't you?

Barry   No.

Gerard   End up on the cutting-room floor.

Barry   Well Ewan said he'd ask the writers to try and expand it.

Gerard   So you're sitting in the back of a freezing dirty van for three months waiting to be called. Then act your guts out for thirteen identical takes, till you're ready to tear off your face. Then you turn up for the premier and find your part's been hacked to bits or cut out altogether. Don't even bother to tell you. Sit there humiliated with your mates sniggering: 'So quick I missed you.' Or: 'So good I didn't know it was you.' Alternatively get the support and stimulus of a united band of actors and the love and excitement of a live audience for several weeks. Know what I'd prefer.

Barry   You really hacked off with me then?

Gerard   I perfectly understand you're tempted.

Barry   But I'll surely get another chance to start my theatre career, won't I?

Gerard   What do you mean 'start'?

Barry   Well eh obviously I'd have to give up Alloa. Well, I would, wouldn't I? The times clash.

Gerard   Give up Alloa?

Barry   Yes.

Gerard   Give up Alloa?

Barry   Well yes, Gerard. What else could I do?

Gerard   You can't give up the Wee Theatre in Alloa. They're a very powerful organisation. You'd never work again in Scotland.

Barry   Aw don't say that. I've always wanted to say, 'I'd love to come back from Hollywood and work at home again. Of course I would. Particularly if it's theatre. It's my first love, you know.'

Gerard   It's a well-known fact that we Scots would rather empty our theatres with talentless nobodies than make room for international stars. You'll just have to face it, son. You were born into a nation suffering from chronic success resentment.

Barry   Well I guess I'll just have to make that sacrifice then. But you will still mentor me, won't you?

Gerard   Are you suggesting I should mentor someone that puts big bucks and film before pennies and theatre?

Barry   Oh fuck. Oh God. I'm gutted now. Gerard Galston
or Ewan Carlyle. Film or theatre. Scotland or the whole wide
world. Why does life have to be so hard on an innocent
young actor? And why oh why did I have to be born
Scottish? I'm so unlucky!

Gerard   I wouldn't mind, but I only agreed to do the
fuckin' job because of you.

Barry   You did not! You /? Seriously?

Gerard   Why else would I go to bloody Alloa? I was that
much away from joining the RSC at one point, you know.

Barry   Wow. I can't believe that. Wow. I've always wanted
someone to say that. 'I want to work with Barry Barr. I've
heard he's a very generous actor.' Thank you, Gerard.
Thank you so much.

Gerard   And I know Jeremy Jennings thinks very highly
of you.

Barry   Does he? I mean does he really?

Gerard *nods significantly.*

Barry   So I did well in the audition then?

Gerard   Oh no.

Barry   No?

Gerard   Apparently you spoke in a mumbling monotone.
And you paused.

Barry   Is that bad?

Gerard   Shakespeare never pauses. Well would you like
to sit in an audience and listen to (*Mumbling and pausing.*)
'Tomorrow . . . and tomorrow . . . and tomorrow . . .
creeps in . . . this petty pace . . . till the last syllable . . .
of . . . ?

Barry   Well, that was how Ewan Carlyle did it.

Gerard   Ewan Carlyle has never performed Shakespeare
in his life.

Barry He came to the college and gave a demonstration. Said don't listen to your tutors. Do Shakespeare your own way and make it real.

Gerard If the audience want real they can stand in the middle of Sauchiehall Street and watch the cops and the touts, the students and the winos, the traffic wardens and the hairy marys, the neds and the gallus alices, the taxi drivers and the drug traffickers, the eaters and the drinkers and the standers-around and starers: it's all there. Shakespeare wrote poetic drama and he *never* pauses.

Barry So why did Jeremy want me then if I'm so crap?

Gerard Lured by your raw untutored explosive talent.

Barry Did he say that about me? Wow, man, wow. But what am I gonny say to Ewan?

Gerard He'll congratulate you.

Barry For turning down a part in his film?

Gerard For being your own man. And if he doesn't congratulate you, he's a dishonourable rogue who should be blacklisted from the profession. Off you go.

Barry Right, Gerard. I will. I'll go right round there and tell him.

Barry *goes to go.*

Gerard Oh, Barry, son.

Barry *stops in his tracks*

Gerard You know those radio ads you've been doing?

Barry Yes?

Gerard Did you get paid all right?

Barry Oh, well, I've not actually had any money yet. Why?

Gerard Just thought I should warn you, some of these people can be a bit /

Barry I'll get it all right. Don't worry. Ace bloke, Hamish. Excellent. Sure you don't want to do one?

Gerard I just want to make sure you get paid. I am your −

Barry Oh, you're not going to say anything to him? I mean, thanks and everything. But I don't want the guy getting annoyed thinking I don't trust him.

Gerard I'll leave it to you what to do.

Barry OK. And thanks for thinking about me. What a truly great mentor you are. I'm so lucky. Cheers. Better get off and break the news to Ewan then.

Gerard Yes, you should.

Barry . . . But I don't know what I'm going to say.

Gerard 'If 'twere done when 'tis done, then 'twere well 'twere done quickly.'

Barry Can't believe I'm turning down a part with Ewan Carlyle, all the same. (*Going out chanting under his breath.*) Can't believe it. Can't believe it. Totally one hundred per cent cannot believe it.

Barry *goes out.* **Gerard** *settles to eat. Gives up in disgust. Scrapes the food into the bin. Goes to go. Thinks better of it and chucks the plate in the bin too, then flounces out.*

Blackout.

Interval.

Scene Five

An hour later. **Maureen** *comes in, looks to flat for* **Dorothy**. *A fax comes through.* **Maureen** *goes over and takes it out, but* **Dorothy** *comes in and distracts her from it.*

Dorothy   Where is she then?

Maureen   Sorry, Dorothy. I'm really sorry.

Dorothy   Och what are you sorry for? I told you it would be London all along, did I not?

Maureen   Eh well actually /

Dorothy   I could have warned her about the drugs menace. I could have warned her about the prostitution. I could have warned her about the lure of the pornographic film industry.

Maureen   Oh but Dorothy /

Dorothy   In a city that eats money these are very real temptations for an impoverished young actress. But your Aunty Dorothy isn't the controlling type, dear. Let your actors follow their mad whims. Let them find out for themselves, she always says.

Maureen   Yes but the thing is /

Dorothy   And I can't see them going for Candice in London. Give it another couple of days. Maximum. All that language. They'll be like 'Who's this foul-mouthed Caledonian freak we've got in our midst?' No, no. Back by the end of the week. You mark my words. Were you attempting to speak, dear?

Maureen   Well I don't actually know if Candice is in London, Dorothy.

Dorothy   You have so much to learn, dear. Where else could she be?

Maureen   You see all that happened was I knocked the door and no one answered.

Dorothy   And how many times did you knock?

Maureen   Eh well once, Dorothy. Ha ha.

Dorothy   Well away back round and knock again. And again. And again! Because an actors' agent is always persistent!

Maureen   Oh ah all right, Dorothy.

Maureen *goes to go with fax.*

Dorothy   Not yet, dear. Honestly you're so impatient. What's in that first? (*Referring to fax.*)

Maureen (*reading*)   'Can you . . . please send on . . . Candice Kilmaurs' CV . . . as she has now . . . signed up . . . with the . . . Pauline Bond Agency of . . . Dean Street, Soho.' . . . What do you think it means?

Dorothy   You nurture these young actresses. You coach them, you're patient through the long barren years, you sweat blood to get them work, you lie through your teeth and what's your reward? Sweet F-all, quite frankly.

Maureen   Do you not want me to send on the details to Pauline then?

Dorothy   Of course you'll send them on. Of course you will. An actors' agent is never petty. Right away please, with our compliments.

Maureen (*going to work*)   Oh right.

Dorothy   Not yet, dear. You're so impatient. First ring Candice on her mobile and tell her to meet Quentin Tarantino at the Ritz in London at one o'clock tomorrow. Say he's wanting to meet her about a part in his new film.

Maureen   Who's Tintin Quarantino?

Dorothy   It's Quentin Tarantino, dear. And he's an international film director.

Maureen   Should we not pass the good news on to Pauline Bongo to tell Candice?

Dorothy   That'll hardly make Candice realise what a foolish wee bitch she's been, giving up her Aunty Dorothy for a London vulture.

Maureen *dials as* **Dorothy** *watches.*

Maureen (*to phone*)   Candice. Aunt Maureen here phoning from Sauchiehall Street. Hope you're all right in London and eh . . . eh . . . that you're not tempted by the / by the / eh / . . .

Dorothy *signals* **Maureen** *to get to the point.*

Maureen (*to phone*)   Because / Because we want you to go to eh / eh / Where was it, Dorothy?

Dorothy *grabs the phone.*

Dorothy (*to phone*)   How could you do this to me, dear? I'm ill with the worry. And not even to face me with it. I've spilt blood for you. I'll have you know I was on the verge of a deal with / with / Well, never mind who I was on the verge of a deal with. Because next time I talk to him you can be sure he won't want to talk to you. So you can shove it up your arse, you backstabbing little cow!

She slams down the phone and bursts into tears as **Maureen** *sits gobsmacked.*

Maureen   Oh, Dorothy. What is it? Are you all right?

Dorothy (*abruptly stops crying*)   What are you talking about? Of course I'm all right.

Dorothy *picks up the phone and presses redial.*

Dorothy (*to phone*)   I'm so sorry, dear. I'm so sorry. You see how badly the worry you've given your Aunty Dorothy makes her behave? But what is it, Candice? Please come back to me. Are you feeling neglected? You're everything to me, you know. Everything. You're the greatest actress of your generation. But you need careful nurturing. And you won't get the attention to detail from these London vultures. With their million-dollar contracts. I am actually on the verge of . . . of . . . well it's big, dear. Very big. And the appeal of London fades quickly. And I swear I'll top myself if you don't come home.

She puts the phone down, bursts into tears and goes to rush out.

Maureen Dorothy.

Dorothy Oh what now, dear?

Maureen You forgot to tell Candice about the meeting tomorrow.

Dorothy Oh, that's right, mock me, why don't you? I'm far too emotional to be an actors' agent. Always have been, always will be. A green young actress. Just a green young actress and I can't even lie to her about a non-existent meeting.

Maureen You mean . : . there is no meeting . . . with Quintin Tarantula?

Dorothy Of course there's no meeting with . . . Quentin Tarantino. To him the Dorothy Darvel Agency is a flea-bitten dump in a regional backwater. If a Hollywood director sees a young actress has a Scottish agent his first assumption is she'll be a talentless waste of space.

Maureen Oh, they don't think that, do they?

Dorothy Of course they think it.

Maureen But it's not actually true, though? Because if all the Scottish actors found out they'd have their feelings hurt. They are children after all. And they'd . . . they'd all want London agents.

Dorothy Oh yes, Maureen. Oh yes. Your well-concealed abilities are beginning to peep through the murk at last. Yes, I'm sorry to say every actor on our books has got this crazy notion they can be a big fish in a big pond. It's set off at the slightest provocation. Against all known laws of statistics. Now get on the phone and tell her about the meeting.

Maureen I will, Dorothy. I will. But eh / I eh /

Dorothy Yes?

Maureen Well if Candice turns up at the Ritz there'll be nobody there to meet her.

Dorothy   Exactly. The poor girl will be so traumatised she'll take the first train back to Scotland into the welcoming arms of her Aunty Dorothy and the Wee Theatre in Alloa.

Maureen (*amazed*)   But do you think I could manage it, Dorothy? When you couldn't?

Dorothy   Och dear, your Aunty Dorothy's past her sell-by date. The world has changed since her day. I remember the time when actors would take their agents out and buy them a drink. Not now though. They think it's your fault if they're out of work for five minutes. You feel like saying, 'It's not my fault you can't act.' But you never do, dear. You just take it on the chin if you're an actors' agent. Yes it's a minefield out there nowadays. For which I naturally assumed you were perfect. Because anyone who can spend the best years of her life hiding from men must be a subhuman little monster. Yes I was stupid enough to think you were perfect to take the Dorothy Darvel Agency into the twenty-first century. But we'll really and truly have to review your position now.

Maureen   But I love working for you, Dorothy. I love being an actors' agent. I love working in the showy world of the glamour business.

Dorothy   Yes but there's such a thing as loving it too much. If you're to be an actors' agent you have to hate your job with every fibre of your being. You have to hate it but still have the stomach to get on with it. In fact, I would go so far as to say you must love hating it.

Maureen   I will try Dorothy. I will. I will try to love hating it. But isn't Alloa a hellhole in the middle of nowhere?

Dorothy   Of course it is, dear. But you must remember some actresses are middle-of-nowhere people. And Candice Kilmaurs is one of them. So if you can get her back home to Scotland I can guarantee your future with the Dorothy Darvel Agency will be secure.

Maureen *waits for a second, then picks up the phone.*

Maureen (*to phone*)   Hello, dear. It's your Aunt Maureen
from Dorothy's office. And just to say that well / well / We've
arranged an interview for you with a Quen . . . tin . . .
Tar . . . an . . . tin . . . o at the Ritz in London at one
o'clock tomorrow for the lovely part of . . . of . . . for a
lovely part in his forthcoming film. Well I hope you're not
having too miserable a time as a prostitute in London. And
don't forget I'll be waiting here with open arms to welcome
you home where I'm having a wonderful time loving hating
being an agent. Ha ha.

She puts phone down, overcome.

Dorothy   Well done, dear. Very well done. And don't
worry. The self-hatred will soon pass. Just think of the
triumph when Candice walks in in floods of tears. Now your
Aunty Dorothy's just popping out for an hour. And she's
secure in the knowledge she's leaving her agency in your
more than capable hands.

Dorothy *goes out, beaming.* **Maureen** *sits stunned.*

Gerard *comes in, from flat. He double-takes a few times.*

Gerard   What's the matter with your face?

Maureen   Oh, nothing. I'm very happy. I'm just taking
the Dorothy Darvel agency into the twenty-first century.

Gerard   And what does that involve exactly?

Maureen   Just learning to love hating my job and putting
a stop to these actresses stabbing me and Dorothy in the
back and running off to the / to the / to the loo of the
pomegranate film industry!

Gerard   Oh she's got you ruining people's careers has she?

Maureen   But London isn't good for these young actresses.
Don't forget the fantasy about being small and getting found
in a big pish.

Gerard   What about the lure of reaching your potential
and getting fulfilling, demanding work with other great
talents in the greatest capital city in the world? He who is

tired of London is tired of life, as they say. Everyone who wants to reach the top of their particular tree *has* to go to London. I had the chance to go myself, you know. But would Dorothy join me? 'Turn down the RSC and I'll be pregnant within the year,' she says. Then it was, 'We'll start a family next year once I've got the business on it's feet.' And it was the same thing year after year till it was . . till it was . . So now every time I pass a boy in the street I'm thinking the son I never had!

Maureen Well I'm sure Dorothy did eh . . . what she did with the best of /

Gerard . . . What? . . . With the best of what?

Maureen Just that . . . just that . . . Well she wouldn't want you to get hurt when the critics / when the critics /

Gerard When the critics what?

Maureen Eh . . . eh . . . well she was probably just . . . trying to stop your fanny getting a good panning . . . You know?

Gerard Oh don't make excuses for her. She was too scared to go to London and risk being a small fish in a big pond, as I believe you were trying to say. Too terrified the London vultures would have her for breakfast. Just because Dorothy says she's quite happy up a close at the wrong end of Sauchiehall Street doesn't mean everyone else has to be.

Maureen But Dorothy's quite critical of the modern Sauchiehall Street and all the outsize pizzas. She recalls fondly the French department stores where everyone could . . . speak French, was it?

Gerard Don't let the old girl fool you. Sauchiehall Street was never like that in Dorothy's lifetime. When she was starting up it was all unisex hair salons, psychedelic disco-theques and concrete shopping malls. So if you've got any sense you'll get out now.

Maureen Oh I can't get out now. I love being an actors' agent.

Gerard Nonsense. You could go to London and be an actors' agent. No problem.

Maureen I don't think so, Gerard. The London sculptures would have me for breakfast.

Gerard All right! But if you must stick around you won't ruin people's careers like Dorothy, will you?

Maureen Eh . . . /

Gerard Will you, Maureen?

Maureen Eh no. I won't. Of course not.

After a second **Maureen** *picks up the phone and dials.*

Maureen *(to phone)* Oh Candice, dear. It's your Aunt Maureen. Just to say your wee meeting with Qu / Qu / Qu / with you know who has been . . . postponed till / till / I'll get back to you as soon as I know more.

She puts the phone down.

Gerard Well done, Maureen. You be an agent in your own way and cock a snook at my wife. Ha ha. She's got it coming to her. Trust me.

Maureen Oh I could never trust you. You like having your cock sucked.

Gerard *double-takes a couple of times.*

Gerard Now listen here, young lady. What exactly are you trying to / ?

A fax comes through noisily. **Maureen** *goes over and reads it.*

Maureen It's Alloa. They're saying you've . . . eh well you've not got the part, but that they hope you can work together some time in the –

Gerard What? That's rubbish. Must be a mistake. *(He grabs the fax from her and races through it and picks up the phone and dials. To phone.)* Jeremy Jennings, please? . . .

Barry *comes in unseen.*

Gerard Well, can you tell him when you see him I'm not interested in the *Macbeth* job. Sorry. . . . Gerard Galston . . . Oh I didn't? Easy to say that now. Oh, and can you also suggest next time he's sucking his own cock, do himself a favour and bite it off? . . . I said: tell him to /

Gerard *realises they have hung up and puts the phone down.*

Barry You're not doing Alloa?

Gerard No I'm not. And don't try and persuade me. And if you've got any sense you'll turn it down too.

Barry . . . Oh that's brilliant. Totally amazing. Wow.

Gerard What?

Barry Well, I'm not taking it either. Well when I told Ewan what you said about film being a form of pornography he said that was total and utter bollocks.

Gerard And did he bother to say why?

Barry Well, actually no. But he said he'd ask one of the producers and get back to me.

Gerard And that satisfied you, did it?

Barry Well yes. Well no. Well, I don't know whether it does or not till he talks to that producer, do I? So then I said I was going to the Wee Theatre instead of doing his film. So he said no one in their right mind would ever work in Alloa. So then I said, 'OK then, I won't, Ewan.' So then I told him about you. And *even though* he's never actually heard of you he said you sounded great and he wants you to be in the film too. What a guy, eh?

Gerard I beg your pardon?

Barry Well, he wants to meet you first, of course.

Gerard I'd rather die.

Barry But you don't understand. It's a totally different film now. And with me playing a totally different part.

Gerard   And what does he want you to play? Saddam himself?

Barry   Oh no. Not at all. It's actually *Macbeth*.

Gerard   Come again? He wants *you* to play *Macbeth* in his film about *Saddam Hussein*?

Barry   Wow, man, eh? Yes, Ewan's going to have a touring Shakespeare company going round Iraq before the war when Saddam was still top man. And I'd play Macbeth and you'd play King Duncan and all three witches and the director! The idea is, it would be a really small company. And you know what? I think it all came from me talking to him about you and your lifelong love of Shakespeare. Well? What do you think?

Gerard   Completely unbelievable. The Iraquis would never have allowed it. They'd think the play was an attack on them.

Barry   That's the whole idea. You know: that the touring company would be getting like totally harassed by the Iraqui cops in case they're western spies or propaganda guys. When they're actually just a bunch of do-gooders patronising the natives and that. And Ewan's on to the writers to get the screenplay rewritten already. Well?

Gerard   I've already told you my answer.

Barry   But it's actual Shakespeare. And we'd get paid thousands seemingly.

Gerard *looks at* **Barry** *sharply.*

Barry   Of pounds. And he was kind of hinting it would be at least ten.

Beat as **Gerard** *hesitates.*

Dorothy *comes in from street.*

Dorothy   I've done it, dear. I've done it.

Gerard   What?

Dorothy   Flight to Southampton. Then cruise to New York, Florida, Jamaica, Panama Canal, San Francisco, Honolulu, Sydney Harbour, Perth and Cape Town.

Gerard   No way. No way. No way.

Dorothy   It's all right, Gerard. It's a few weeks away. Alloa'll be done and –

Gerard   I turned Alloa down.

Dorothy   Oh, right. I . . . Well, that's excellent. You're free then.

Gerard   Did you not hear me?

Dorothy   But it was you that wanted a cruise.

Gerard   You cruise if you want. It's a film.

Dorothy   But where are you going to get work? You've offended everyone in Scotland.

Gerard (*shooshing* **Barry**)   I've been offered a part in a film.

Dorothy   You don't do film.

Gerard   I do when it's Shakespeare. With Ewan Carlyle, the greatest actor of his generation and now director.

Dorothy   But you've been refusing all screen offers for thirty years. You can't start changing now. And the cruise was your idea. You wanted to get the old Dorothy back.

Gerard   I wouldn't go two stops on a bus with you. Ha ha. That'll teach you to open your own bank account, you rancid old slapper.

Dorothy   But I've paid for the trip.

Gerard   Cancel it.

Dorothy   No I will not. I'll lose the deposit!

Gerard *goes to go.*

Dorothy   Gerard, come back here. Gerard. Here. I've got money for you. You won't need to take the job. Gerard!

Gerard   Shove your money up your arse.

Dorothy   How can you talk like that to me, Gerard?

Gerard   Easily.

Gerard *ushers* **Barry** *towards street exit.*

Dorothy   Oh Gerard, don't go. Please don't go. Oh I've got pains. Oh all down my leg. Oh I'll have to sit down. Oh I'm going to pass out. Gerard. Gerard. Gerard!

Gerard *and* **Barry** *have gone.*

Dorothy   Oh, what have I done? What have I done? Oh. Oh. Oh. Oh. Oh. I'll have to go and lie down. Send Gerard to my bedside as soon as he comes in. Repeat: as soon as he comes in, dear! Oh. Oh. Oh. Oh. He'll end up in Hollywood playing subhuman monsters with clipped English accents and shagging C-list actresses and acquire a sexually transmitted disease. Oh. Oh. Oh. Oh. Why has this happened to me, Maureen? Well?

Maureen   Could it be because you . . . ?

Dorothy   Yes?

Maureen   Well because you . . . ?

Dorothy   Yes, Maureen?

Maureen   Well could it possibly be because you kept on promising Gerard children?

Dorothy   What?

Maureen   You know year after year until it was too /

Dorothy   How could he betray me like that? How could he? To you of all people? After all I've done for him. I did it to protect him from the truth, Maureen. He'd have left me if he'd found out. And where would he be without me? Where would he be? Answer me that.

Maureen   Well what did you not want him to find out?

Dorothy   Oh yes. That's you all over, Maureen Mauchline. (*Rage building.*) Dig, dig, dig till you get the dirt. Dig, dig, dig

till you / Are you a woman or a sexless freak? Answer me
that. Are you a woman or a / ? Don't you realise Gerard's
a man? He'd have left me if he found out the real reason
I didn't have his children was I didn't bloody want them!
(*Suddenly pathetic.*) Oh. Oh. Oh. Oh.

Dorothy *goes out, as if in agony. Beat.*

Maureen (*calling after* **Dorothy**)   Oh a positive attitude,
please. A positive attitude at all times. *If* you're to be an
actors' agent.

A fax starts to come through. **Maureen** *is just about to take out the
fax when* **Candice** *comes in.*

Candice   Oh, Maureen. What have I done?

Maureen   Come in and tell your Aunt Maureen.

Candice   I wasn't going to get on the train with Gina.
I really and truly wasn't. But then did she not go and burst
into tears and totally make me go with her. So we spent the
whole journey down in the toilet because I didn't have a
ticket. It was the best laugh I'd had in my life. So I was
totally intending getting the first train back but when we get
off at London Gina starts crying again and totally makes me
go up the road with her to her bedsitter. Then the next day
I've to go round all the agencies with her. Into this Pauline
Bond's place. Only she's got it all mixed up, stupid bitch.
Thought it was me that was applying. And what a cow as
well. She said I looked regional. So I told her to fuck off,
I wasn't interested. But she made me sign up with her
anyway because though I'm raw I've got potential. But she
soon changed her tune. I mean: only in London a few days
and it's could I please stop plaguing her at her office? Well,
I never got that off Dorothy. And not a single audition in
five whole days. What's the point of being in London if
you're not earning any money? You're just shelling out
hunners and hunners of pounds for fuck all. Then I get
off the train and get all these mad messages off you about
Quentin Tarantino or something. You've to go, you've not
to go. You'd think someone that thinks up all those shootings

could make up his fuckin' mind about a meeting. And now I feel like I should get back on the train and apologise to Pauline Bond for messing her about and making a total tit of myself. Even though I hate the snobby bitch's guts. And now Dorothy'll never have me back after what I done to her. (*Aggressive suddenly.*) Will she?

Maureen Oh, don't worry. I'm running the agency now. So I'm sending you over to the Wee Theatre in Alloa. I've lined you up the lovely part of / of / of / in their forth-coming production of / of / of /

Candice But is Alloa not in the middle of nowhere somewhere? I've never heard of it.

Maureen Exactly.

Candice What do you mean, exactly? Exactly what?

Maureen Well, you're a middle-of-nowhere person. Alloa will be perfect for you. There won't be millions of people you don't know. Less than thirty. Off you go now. Getting the bus to Alloa is like your Aunt Maureen. A daring deed.

Candice I really like you, Maureen.

Maureen I like you too, Candice.

Candice You've got a totally amazing insight into my character. 'Middle-of-nowhere person.' That is so true. And I've always wanted to know who I am!

Candice *goes.* **Maureen** *stretches up to her full height and goes over to* **Dorothy**'s *desk. She farts around for a second like a child then slowly sits at the desk. A fax comes through. She goes over to read it. Then goes back to the phone.*

Maureen (*to phone*) Hello . . . Oh right. Is that Pauline Bond herself –? In person –? . . . Well, can you tell her she's sent a fax through. It's about a vacancy for an agent's assistant . . . Eh, Maureen Mauchline at the Dorothy Darvel Actors' Agency . . . It's been sent by mistake? . . . Yes. Yes, I will bin it. No problem. Bye now.

Maureen *crumples up the fax and bins it. Beat. After a second she takes it back out and reads it with care.*

Blackout.

Scene Six

Couple of weeks later. **Gerard** *onstage, coaching* **Barry.**

Barry
    If 'twere . . . done when 'tis . . . done
    Then 'twere . . . well 'twere . . . done quickly.

Gerard   Still leaving little pauses in there.

Barry   I'm not. Am I?

Gerard *nods.*

Barry   Fuck. I could've sworn. /

Gerard (*mimicking* **Barry**)
    If 'twere . . . done when 'tis . . . done
    Then 'twere . . .

Barry   But there's a whole massive speech after it. When am I supposed to breathe?

Dorothy (*off*)   Gerard, Gerard!

Barry   What's that?

Gerard   Never mind what that is. Take a deep breath before you start, then snatch a little breath at the end of each line.

Barry (*deep gasp, then*)
    If 'twere done when 'tis done. (*Big gasp.*)
    Then 'twere well 'twere done quickly. (*Big gasp.*)
    If the assassination could trammel up the consequence.
    (*Big gasp.*)

Gerard   Good. Now just hide the breath.

Barry   What do you mean?

Gerard   Breathe in silence or else the audience will be worried you're about to hyperventilate.

Dorothy   Gerard! Bring me in a couple of painkillers!

Gerard   I know what I'll bring you.

Barry   What is that?

Gerard   Work!

Barry
If 'twere done when 'tis done
Then 'twere well 'twere done quickly.

Gerard   That's good. Very good. Just a bit monotonous.

Barry   But it's Shakespeare. Is it not meant to be monotonous?

Gerard   You need to avoid monotony so the audience will absorb the meaning without effort.

Dorothy (*off*)   Gerard! I'm in agony. Gerard! Where are you?

Barry   Is that Dorothy?

Gerard   What if it is? So if you'll start by finding the pattern in the rhythm.

Barry   What?

Gerard   The repetition of the 'tweres. Stress them.

Barry (*overdoing it*)   If *'twere* done when 'tis done then *'twere* well *'twere* done quickly.

Gerard   Yes, but lightly.

Barry   Och I can't do this. There's too many things to think about.

Gerard   You haven't digested it yet. That's all. It'll soon be second nature.

Barry   But it's a massive big part and there's hundreds of massive big speeches and scenes and more and more lines and /

Dorothy *comes in, bedraggled in night-clothes, no make-up.*

Barry Aaaaah. Who's that?

Dorothy It's just your Aunty Dorothy, son. In the raw. What's the matter? Have you never seen a shipwrecked old crone before? Where's that bitch Maureen Mauchline? Punctual, I said to her. Punctual at all times.

Gerard She's visiting her mother twice a day these days. Apparently the end is nigh. Now could you clear off and give us all peace.

Dorothy I'm ill Gerard. I'm aching all over. I'm sweating. My hand's been shaking. My teeth are rattling.

Gerard Then take them out.

Dorothy It's not funny. I feel like I might die.

Gerard Then away back to your deathbed. With any luck you will. Come on Barry.

Dorothy Oh, don't go Gerard. I'm sorry. If only / I just /

Gerard What is it now, woman?

Dorothy I just wish you'd change your mind about the cruise, Gerard. Well we could still go. It's the Wednesday after next. It would be an excellent chance for us to get back on the rails. You said as much yourself.

Gerard No, no, no, no, no. And that's final.

Dorothy As soon as we hit the Atlantic I'll be an angel. You'll get the old Dorothy back. I'll re-open the bedroom door.

Gerard Yes but I won't be there to enter it. And face facts. Whole holiday'd be ruined you worrying about your precious agency.

Dorothy Oh ho ho. I can assure you Maureen Mauchline is more than capable of running the place.

Gerard I wouldn't be too sure about that. She'll be offering to suck every cock that walks in the door.

Dorothy   Och, nonsense, dear. She thinks a cock's something you find in a farmyard. Ha ha ha.

Gerard   How wrong can you be? Now if you could let Barry and me get back to /

Dorothy   What do you mean by that?

Gerard   Oh never mind.

Dorothy   No, Gerard. What do you −?

Gerard   Come on Barry. We'll go and work at the /

Dorothy   Gerard! What . . . do . . . you . . . mean by / ?

Gerard   I mean Dorothy: she offered to suck mine!

Dorothy   . . . Are you sure it wasn't you that offered to let her?

Gerard   When it comes to casual blow-jobs it's under-twenty-fives only, I'm afraid.

Dorothy   I knew it. I knew she was a little slut from the minute she walked in the door. And to think I took her on, taught her everything I know and made her what she is today. Well, she'll regret that. Oh yes, oh yes, oh yes, oh yes.

Gerard   What are you up to now?

Dorothy   Oh, who knows. Who the hell knows? But Dorothy Darvel is back. With a vengeance, as Shakespeare once said.

Gerard   Shakespeare did not say that.

Dorothy   Oh how do you know? Were you around at the time? He could have said it in private conversation. And who the hell cares who said it? Who the hell cares? Who − the hell − cares?

Dorothy *goes out to flat.*

Gerard   Right. Back to work.

Barry   If 'twere done when 'tis done then 'twere well 'twere done . . . How could you two talk to each other like that? That was shocking. I was shocked. Are you going to tell me that wasn't a shocking way to talk to your wife?

Gerard Work.

Barry If 'twere done when 'tis / But it's all a complete waste of time. Ewan keeps changing it anyway.

Gerard Yes I know. He wants you to ham it up.

Barry It's his film.

Gerard But it's your part. He's only the director, not God. And he wants you to take the piss out of Shakespeare.

Barry Yes so you keep telling him. And if he wants to make the point that what are poncey western actors doing patronising the natives that's up to him, isn't it?

Gerard A completely gratuitous point if you ask me.

Barry Who asked you?

Gerard Well Ewan seems to take it all right.

Barry Yes. Seems to.

Gerard Meaning what?

Barry Well, he's a first-time director. I don't think he'd realised how demanding actors can be.

Gerard I'm not demanding. I'm principled.

Barry You're not that principled.

Gerard What?

Barry Aw, it's all right.

Gerard No come on. Out with it.

Barry Och it doesn't matter.

Gerard Barry!

Barry Well, OK, all right. I went to see that Hamish Hunter guy. To see about the radio money. Like you said.

Gerard Yes and how did you get on?

Barry   I said with it being film it might be a while before we get paid. So I could really do with my money for the ads as soon as.

Gerard   And what did he say?

Barry   He said that's not his problem. So I said my mentor's a very important actor and he said I should come in and demand my money. So he said what actor's this?

Gerard   You didn't tell him?

Barry   Course I told him. Too right. I was trying to put the wind up him. Don't mind, do you?

Gerard   . . . What did he say to that?

Barry   Well, this was where it got weird. He actually said you'd been working for him too . . . So I said, nah there's no way Gerard would do a radio ad. He thinks that's like prostitution. Don't you?

Gerard   . . . Did he say anything else?

Barry   Well. First of all he sort of smirked. Then he said, oh, that's why you'd asked him not to mention it to anyone. So then I thought maybe it *was* you, Gerard.

Gerard   No way.

Barry   Aw, come, man. Admit it. I won't think any less of you.

Gerard   Absolutely not. You know my feelings about that subject.

Barry   Yeah but you have been pushed for cash.

Gerard   I have not and never will do advertising. Now do you want to work or don't you?

Barry   All right. All right. I was only saying because you asked me. Shame all the same. Because next thing the guy bursts out laughing, says sorry for the delay it was just a cashflow problem, opened his wallet and doled out seven hundred quid. (*He takes out the money.*) Five hundred for me and two hundred for you. Will I just take your share back then?

Gerard Eh, no. You're all right.

Barry But it's not your money.

Gerard I'll take it back myself. Well he's obviously got me mixed up with someone else. I'll go round and straighten him out about it.

Barry *hands over the money.* **Gerard** *takes it, counts it and puts it in his wallet.*

Barry It was you, wasn't it? Come on. You can tell me.

Gerard Can we work?

Barry OK. OK. If 'twere done when 'tis –

Phone goes noisily. They look at it. **Maureen** *breezes in, in black.*

Maureen Hi everybody. Oh, right. Don't answer the phone for me. (*She picks up the phone. To phone:*) Maureen Mauchline here. The Dorothy Darvel Agency . . . Oh hello Pauline . . . Ah huh. Ah huh. (*Etc.*)

Gerard *waves* **Barry** *out with him to street, sharing waves with* **Candice** *as she comes in.*

Maureen (*to phone*) Oh well I don't know if you read my application but I did say that even though this is a flea-bitten slum in a regional back passage I am actually running it these days . . . Oh yes fantastic. Excellent . . . An interview on Tuesday will be fine. . . . Oh no, no problem. . . . Thank you, Pauline. Thank you. Bye now. (*She puts the phone down.*)

Candice (*like a dam bursting on cue*) Oh Maureen, Maureen, Maureen, Maureen, Maureen, Maureen.

Maureen What is it, dear? Come in and tell your Aunt Maureen. Now pull yourself together and I'll give you the three S's. And aren't you supposed to be in Alloa?

Candice I know, Maureen. I know. But that's just it. With me being stuck in Alloa I've totally went and forgot who

I am. Well no wonder. I walked the full length of Alloa High
Street and I didn't meet a single solitary person discussing
Gregory Greig or David Burke! Honest to God, ask any one
of them about the zeitgeist they're like, 'You won't get the
zeitgeist in Alloa. You'll have to go to Stirling for that!' And
as for that Jeremy Jennings, just because he's been to
Cambridge he thinks he can make a cunt of you. On and
on about multinationals and could I act my 'Whither should
I fly' speech like a portent of global warming because all the
glaciers have melted in my Arctic home and I'm desperate
to find somewhere new to live and start another family?
I don't know about you, Maureen. I just feel if my kids have
been murdered a new family'd be the last thing on my
mind. And who needs to act like the globe's getting warmer?
The Wee Theatre's like an oven! Well, seemingly the air
conditioning's so noisy they have to keep it switched off or
the audience can't hear! Then he's got me in his office
telling me I've to act more professional on the one hand
while he's feeling my tits with the other one. Please tell me
I don't have to go back. I just wished I'd stayed in London.
Too late, though, isn't it? Pauline Bond will never have me
back now. Totally lovely as well. Built up my confidence.
Well she didn't. She actually ran it into the ground. But at
least she was the one person who wasn't scared to stand up
and tell me who I am. A raw untutored talent but could
I stop telling people what I think of them? I mean, what's
wrong with mentioning to the girls in her office they look
like they've got a bike pump stuck up their fanny? So do
you think it is too late? Do you, Maureen? (*Aggressive.*) Well
do you?

Maureen   Oh I think when I recommend you to Pauline
Bond a week on Tuesday morning she'll take you back with
open arms.

Candice   But what about walking out on Alloa?

Maureen   Oh you've got *so* much to learn. Don't you
realise that Alloa would read like a pimple on your CD for
many decades to come? You're the greatest actor of your

generation and London is where you must go to reach your full vagina. Because he who is tired of London is tired of shite.

Candice   But what about Dorothy?

Maureen   Don't talk to me about that bitch. Do you realise she made up the whole interview at the Ritz specially to let you rot at the Wee Theatre, in Alloa? She should be barred from the amorous world of showjumping. She should have her arse licked by the profession. She should /

Candice   I can't believe she'd do that to me. Could you kill her for me?

Maureen   That won't be necessary. She lies in bed all day taking heart attacks. Now away home and get ready for the golden showers of London.

Candice   Thanks, Maureen. Thank you so much. Because it's just so excellent to finally meet someone that can stand up and tell me who – the fuck – I am! Yes! Yes! Yes!

Candice *goes chanting as* **Dorothy** *comes in, back to herself.* **Maureen** *beams at* **Dorothy**.

Maureen   Hello, Dorothy. How are you feeling now?

Dorothy   Never mind about me. It's the agency I'm concerned about. How would you say you've been doing?

Maureen   Oh fantastic, Dorothy. Excellent. I would definitely say you left your agency in my more than collapsible hands.

Dorothy   I couldn't agree less. You've got the place overrun with actors, your timekeeping's atrocious, your appearance has deteriorated abominably and you're far too familiar with my husband. You're completely unsuitable to be an actors' agent. So I'm afraid it's two weeks' notice. I know this is disappointing for you. But you won't be able to talk your Aunty Dorothy round. So don't even think about it.

Maureen   Oh, I'd never try and talk you out of two weeks' notice. Because, let's face it, I'm totally unsuitable to work at the wrong end of Sauchiehall Street. Because Sauchiehall Street's never had a French chandelier. Not in your lifetime. Well, has it, Dorothy? No no, I've decided I'm far, far, far too big a pond for a small pish like you.

Dorothy Oh what are you trying to say, girl? How can you ever have expected to be an actors' agent talking like a halfwit?

Maureen Yes but Scottish actors will even go with a halfwit to get a London agent.

Dorothy Yes, but you're not a London agent. You're not even a Scottish agent now. You're nothing but a / Oh, I don't know why I'm bothering. Nothing you say makes the slightest bit of sense. So if you don't mind you can leave now. I will pay you to the end of the month. I can't – of course – offer you a reference, but good luck in your search for alternative employment. Can I suggest Woolworth's shop assistant? Or possibly something less intellectually taxing? Oh, and to show there are no hard feelings on my part, may I ask one last time, how is your mother?

Maureen Well, she actually died last week. The funeral was this morning.

Dorothy Oh, I'm so sorry, dear. And were you with your poor mother at the end?

Maureen Oh yes.

Dorothy And what were her final words?

Maureen Well she actually asked me who I was.

Dorothy I'm so so sorry. And what did you say to that?

Maureen Well, I said: 'It's your daughter, mum. It's Maureen.'

Dorothy So what did she say?

Maureen Em, um, she actually said, em, 'You're not my daughter. You're a . . . cunting bastard. Now get to fuck out of it and don't come back.'

Dorothy I'm so so sorry, dear. I'm so so /

Maureen Oh why? It was a thoroughly joyous occasion.
I kissed the ballbearers and showered the coffin with confetti.

Dorothy Well, may God forgive your callous treatment of
an old lady that scrimped and saved to bring you into the
world. I mean: happy at your own mother's funeral, dear.
How could you?

Maureen Well, I'd just found out how much she left me.

Dorothy That's shocking behaviour, Maureen. Shocking.
Was it a generous legacy? Region of forty or fifty thousand,
perhaps? Or pushing sixty possibly?

Maureen Oh no. It was actually £324,000. And I was
thinking of offering it to you for the agency. Just as well
I didn't though, eh? With me being so unsuitable.

Dorothy *looks like she's about to faint.*

Maureen Are you all right? Not taking another heart
attack are you? Well, I'm sure you'll recover. So bye now,
Dorothy. Bye and thanks for /

Dorothy Oh Maureen there's no need to go.

Maureen It's no problem me going. I'm only too happy
to /

Dorothy Maybe I was a bit hasty. I . . . I didn't realise it
was your mother's funeral today. Time off is the least you
could expect. Please stay.

Maureen No, I think I'll just stick with your previous
offer. I liked the previous offer better. I'll go now, if you
don't mind.

Dorothy (*grabbing* **Maureen**) Please stay, dear. For your
Aunty Dorothy. You know I've not been well.

Maureen Oh get off me, you virginal back passage in a
flea-bitten bum, as someone once said.

Maureen *shakes* **Dorothy** *off.*

Dorothy   I'm so sorry, dear. I'm so sorry. I don't know what I was thinking of. And do call round any time. Any time, dear.

Maureen   Oh, I don't think I'll be calling round. You don't want your office cluttered with out-of-work agents.

Dorothy   Oh but I insist. We could even discuss you buying my list off me. I won't be hard to deal with. I think you'll find I'll sell at a rock-bottom price.

Maureen   Oh hard to get, Dorothy. Hard to get at all times. If you're to be an actors' agent. If you're to be an actors' agent. If you're to be an actors' agent.

Maureen *goes chanting into the distance as* **Dorothy** *watches her go, then faints.*

Scene Seven

A couple of weeks later.

Dorothy *at desk. Phone rings. She picks it up.*

Dorothy (*to phone*)   Dorothy Darvel Agency . . . Maureen Mauchline is no longer employed here . . . No, I don't have a mobile number for her . . . Yes, it is . . . Is that you, Candice? How are you, dear? . . . Well, there's no need for language . . . I did nothing of the kind. Certainly not . . . I'm not discussing this on the phone. If you'd like to come into the office I'd be only too . . .

Dorothy *realises* **Candice** *has hung up and puts the phone down. Beat.* **Gerard** *comes in from street, stunned.*

Dorothy   Back early, dear? Weren't you supposed to be on the set all day?

Gerard *sinks into a chair, not responding to her.*

Dorothy   Is there something wrong, Gerard? . . . Gerard, what is it? . . . Gerard if you're back drinking I'll / As if I didn't have enough on my plate. That Maureen Mauchline's been poisoning Candice Kilmaurs' ears about me. I'm doomed to be misunderstood till my dying day . . . All right, Gerard. You can't sit around the office in that state. Gerard! . . . And you know what's happening this afternoon, don't you? Our flight is leaving for Southampton. Without us. That's thousands of my hard-earned pounds getting poured into the Atlantic. Are you listening to me, Gerard? Gerard!

Barry *rushes in from street and up to* **Gerard**.

Barry Well, I hope you're sorry, you / you / you old fart!

Dorothy Don't you talk like that to my husband. Can't you see he's unwell?

Barry How, what's wrong with him?

Dorothy *comes over.*

Dorothy (*ushering* **Barry** *away*) If you'd get away from him I might find out.

Barry *retreats.*

Dorothy What is it, Gerard? What is it?

Barry This can't be happening to me. Can it? Not to me. I'm young and innocent and just starting out on life's journey and / Well, this was supposed to be my big break and / So I go into Ewan's office, right? Just for a chat. To say how much I'm enjoying myself, how much I appreciate the opportunity and if he's got any suggestions how I can be even better and / well, he's not even there! But his assistant director is there and she's like / Well, she's really sorry but my part's been cut from the film. I'm like, but it's one of the main parts. She's like, she's really really sorry but they decided the touring theatre company was completely unbelievable and it was coming over like they were taking the piss out of Shakespeare so they cut it. I'm like, well can I at least get my original part back as Saddam's nephew? She's like, it was recast the week before. (*Referring to* **Gerard**.) And it's all his fault we got the push. It was him that kept having a go at Ewan.

Dorothy   Well, a serious artist has to stand up for what he believes in, dear.

Barry   And as for all that stuff about film being a form of pornography? Well Ewan's producer got back to Ewan and said that in the olden times that's what people used to say about Shakespeare.

Dorothy   I think you'll find that there are enemies of art and enlightenment in every age, dear. No, no. My husband may have his faults but he does have his principles.

Barry   Principles his arse, Dorothy. Principles his arse. Principles his big fat arse!

Barry *takes out a tape and goes to play it.*

Dorothy   I've got an agency to run, dear. So if you don't mind, could you leave now, please.

Barry   What do you mean leave? How can I just leave? You'll have to phone up and get my part back first.

Dorothy   That won't be possible.

Barry   Well what about my contract?

Dorothy   Oh well they will still have to pay you. I'll look your contract out later and get back to you.

Barry   I don't care about the money. Can you not just get me my job back?

Dorothy   Sorry.

Barry   Well why not?

Dorothy   Well you see, dear, in the glamorous world of show business having your part cut's just a kind way of saying they don't like your acting.

Barry   But I'm one of the most talented actors of my generation.

Dorothy   And who told you that?

Barry   Oh only Ewan Carlyle! Remember?

Dorothy   Sounds like he's changed his mind.

Barry   Well, can you get on the phone and get me something else then?

Dorothy   I can't, no.

Barry   Well, what's the point of you being my agent?

Dorothy   I wanted to talk to you about that.

Barry   Oh, OK? What is it?

Dorothy   I'm letting you go. Sorry.

Barry   Oh, you're not, are you? . . . You can't.

Dorothy   Well it sounds like you're a bit of a disappointment to our Ewan. And I've got the reputation of my agency to consider.

Barry   But I haven't done anything wrong. (*Referring to* **Gerard**.) It was him.

Dorothy   Sorry. I have my standards.

Barry   Oh, please don't do that . . . Please. My dad'll . . . He'll . . .

Dorothy   You're never worried your father will kill you?

Barry   Oh, it's much worse that that. He'll say . . . (*Breaking down.*) I . . . told . . . you . . . so . . . prick! (*He starts bawling.*)

Dorothy   Oh, for God's sake. Pull yourself together. This is an actors' agency, not a daytime talk show. Away and clean yourself up.

Barry   Sorry, Dorothy, I'm really sorry. I'm really really sorry.

Barry *rushes out to flat.*

Dorothy   Where do you think you're going? Come back here. That's private property. I said: come back here. Gerard. This is all your fault. You made that boy feel too

much at home. He was supposed to be your mentee. Not
the son you never / you never / you never /

Maureen (*in battered coat and hat concealing a makeover*) *rushes in,
seemingly distraught.*

Maureen Oh, Dorothy. I'm so sorry. I'm so, so sorry to
disturb you. But you did say I could call round any time.
And I didn't know who else to turn to in my hour of need.

Dorothy Oh, you know you'll always be welcomed with
open arms at your Aunty Dorothy's. Come away in and tell
me all about it.

Maureen Sure you don't mind?

Dorothy Bitterness is for the hapless amateur, dear.

Maureen Well the interview with Pauline went like a wet
dream.

Dorothy Ah! So you're another one then. When I think of
the intensive coaching I put in to bring you up to the
required standard. The betrayal, the disrespect, the sheer
ingratitude!

Maureen Oh but I'm very grateful, Dorothy. After all,
when I sat down in Pauline's office and she asked me why
I thought I could make an agent I was able to tell her! I said
never tell actors the truth, be hard to get at all times, never
admit you're in the wrong and most important of all never
ever say shat the bed. Well Pauline looked so interested I
decided to even tell her about the three S's. Which was great
because she hadn't actually heard of them. Yes, celery,
scallops and sausage, I said. Ha ha. Well she must have been
impressed because then she said she normally made applicants
wait for an answer but in my case she'd make an exception!
And that she was sorry to say she didn't think I was suitable
to be an actors' agent. Well I was thoroughly gobstopped.
But I managed to blurt out a why. So she said my image
was all wrong. So I said, well what kind of image would you
like. So she said what it was. And it was this.

Maureen *takes her hat and coat off to reveal a decidedly more modern image than* **Dorothy** *gave her. Sharply fashionable but dignified and high-status.*

So I said, well, I think I could change my image to suit. So she said her answer would still be no. So I said, why. So she said, well, please take this the right way, but she didn't understand a word I said. I talked like a halfwit. Well, don't worry, I said, being a halfwit agent was no bar to attracting Scottish actors. As long as you're based in London. So she said, sadly she didn't only deal in Scottish actors but that it's not just what I say that's the problem, it's also the amount. She said to be a successful actors' agent I need to learn to hold a few things back and to think before I speak. So I said did she think I had no future as an agent in London? So she said, probably not unless I had the money to set up on my own. And you know Dorothy, I had the feeling Pauline thought there's no way I'd have the money. And so then she thanked me very much for coming and I was out the door.

Dorothy Well, not to worry, dear. You've now had your first experience of a London vulture and you'll have learnt your lesson. Luckily for you your Aunty Dorothy's very understanding and she will take you back this time as long as you apologise and admit you were in the wrong.

Maureen Oh I could *never* do that, Dorothy.

Dorothy Why on earth not?

Maureen Because an actors' agent never admits they're in the wrong. Everyone would think my actors were a talentless waste of paste. Because London is where the most talented people go to reach their full dementia. Isn't that right, Gerard?

Gerard What's that? What?

Dorothy Yes, but London's decided you're not suitable, Maureen. So it's come back to your Aunty Dorothy or face the wilderness alone, I'm afraid.

Maureen   Well, I was actually wondering if you would still consider selling your list to me.

Dorothy   Well . . . that would depend very much on the /

Gerard   Yes, do it. Do it. Sell your list.

Dorothy   What, dear?

Gerard   We'll go on that cruise. We'll get to know each other again. We'll go and never never never come back.

Dorothy   Oh, do you mean it?

Gerard   I do. Because you know what? I love you.

Dorothy (*overwhelmed*)   Well, I love you too, Gerard. Very much. Very very much. But maybe we should find out how much Maureen wants to pay first. Well, dear?

Maureen   How much would you accept?

Dorothy   I think all in all 200K possibly? And cheap at the price, I might add.

Maureen   I was thinking maybe a bit less.

Dorothy   I could come down a bit, I suppose. Seeing it's you. A hundred and eighty, perhaps?

Maureen   A bit less, I think.

Dorothy   Well . . . All right . . . I can't believe I'm doing this. But a hundred and fifty-five, and that's my last.

Maureen (*getting steely*)   Less.

Dorothy   No I'm sorry, dear. A hundred and fifty-five was the lowest I could −

Gerard   Oh, get real. That's far too much.

Dorothy   Whose side are you on?

Gerard   Meet the girl in the middle.

Dorothy   What middle? Maureen hasn't suggested a figure. There is no middle.

Gerard   If you love me you'll take less.

Dorothy I, eh . . . I, eh . . . My husband wants me to sell at a silly price. So OK, a hundred and thirty-five, and that has to be my last –

Maureen Less, Dorothy.

Gerard Yes less, Dorothy. Take less. ·

Dorothy All right. All right. A hundred and twenty-five, OK? A hundred and twenty-five and it's a done deal.

Maureen You couldn't come down a bit further? I'm saving for my retirement cruise.

Dorothy This is getting ridiculous, Maureen. Could you not just play fair and give me a ballpark of how much you could go to?

Maureen I was actually thinking maybe / . . . well nothing, Dorothy.

Dorothy Come again. What exactly do you mean by / ?

Maureen Oh, you know: nothing! Zero. Sweet F-all.

Dorothy Oh, now you are joking.

Maureen Oh no. I'm not joking. I thought you could just give it to me.

Gerard Yes! Yes! Just give it to her! We'll go and get ready.

Dorothy What are you talking about? I can't just give it to her. I – /

Maureen Oh, that's a shame.

Dorothy And why's that?

Maureen Because if you don't give me it, I think I'll just take it anyway.

Dorothy Oh now, dear. This is getting beyond a joke. Please leave my office.

Gerard Come and get ready, Dorothy.

Dorothy Leave my office now, dear, please. Or –

Maureen Oh, I'm not leaving without your list. So give me it.

Dorothy Oh oh oh oh. This is ridiculous. You have no future as an actors' agent while you're behaving like a desperado. Leave now or I'll call the /

Gerard Come and get ready. Or we'll miss the plane.

Dorothy I eh . . . I eh . . .

Gerard This is our last chance to get to know each other again, Dorothy. It's now or never.

Dorothy Well all right, dear. All right. All right. (*To* **Maureen**.) And you make sure you're gone by the time we're ready to go.

Dorothy *and* **Gerard** *go to go.* **Barry** *comes back in drying his eyes.*

Dorothy And that goes for you too!

Barry What are you talking about now?

Dorothy That goes for you too, I said.

Dorothy *and* **Gerard** *go out to flat.* **Maureen** *goes into her bag, takes out an envelope, from which she takes out an A4 sheet of paper, typed. She goes to the fax and starts feeding it in.*

Barry You'll never guess what today is.

Maureen (*working at fax*) What's that?

Barry The worst day of my young life! I mean I'm young and innocent and just starting out on life's journey and I've lost my job, I've lost my agent, I've lost my / my / What else have I lost? It'll come back to me. Eh eh. What is it again? This is so embarrassing. Oh yes I've lost my mentor. Oh no. I've lost my mentor and he was showing me everything he knew and he was the great Gerard Galston and it's just all so unfair!

Maureen   Yes, you're the greatest actor of your generation.
There's no doubt about it.

Barry   Am I? Do you really think so?

Maureen   After the performance you've just given?

Barry   What performance?

Maureen   All that cock and bullshit about losing this, that
and the other. You can't kid your Aunt Maureen, you know.
All the most talented actors lie through their tits and believe
every word of it.

Barry   But I'm not lying. I have lost my –

Maureen   Oh, don't worry about that. I'll take you on.

Barry   How can you take me on? You don't make the
decisions.

Maureen   Oh, but I do. You see, I'm investing my mother's
gangrenous legacy to rent a London office. Now will you
shut the fuck up a minute while your Aunt Maureen
concentrates. Start. (*She presses.*) Circularise. (*She presses.*) Go.
(*She presses.*) There. So. Are you accepting my offer or aren't
you?

Barry   Well eh yes. But do I have to move to London? Bit
expensive isn't it?

Maureen (*taking out cheque book*)   As a one-off I'll give you
two K for resettlement expenses. Yes or no?

Barry   Eh ah yes.

Maureen *writes cheque.*

Maureen   Now this is on the strict understanding that it
will be paid back out of your first earnings in London.
Because an actor is never a sponge cake. (*She hands it over.*)

Barry   Two thousand. I can't believe it. Two thousand.
Yipedeedoodah. This is the best day of my young life.

Maureen   Yes, but are you ready to go?

Barry Of course. Because I'm young and innocent and just starting out on life's journey and already I've sidestepped all the crap that's totally been getting in the way of me getting up where I /

Maureen On you come, then.

Barry Not need to wait for an answer from your fax first?

Maureen Oh no. I'm expecting over two hundred. We'd be here all day. Come on.

Barry But I have to say goodbye to Gerard. He was a world-class mentor and taught me everything I know.

Maureen And why do you think he did that?

Barry Out of the goodness of his heart. And well actually because he likes me.

Maureen (*patronising*) Oh, you have so much to learn. Did you not know Dorothy had to pay him to do that for you?

Barry Aw no. No way. I don't believe that.

Maureen I saw the money change hands with my own eyes.

Barry Oh fuck. Oh fuck. Oh fuck. Oh fuck. You've gutted me now. I'm so unlucky. Why does it always have to be me? Why did I have to get the worst mentor in the whole wide world? Why? Why? Why? Why? Why? Why? Why? Why? Why? Why? (*Etc.*)

Every time we think he's stopped, he carries on going into sotto voce *when* **Candice** *comes in.*

Candice (*to* **Maureen**) Where – the fuck – have you been? I've been phoning you and phoning you and phoning you. You promised me you were taking me to London to Pauline Bond's.

Maureen Oh she's not interested in you.

Candice No? Well, I'm not interested in her, the snobby cow. What's wrong with me?

Maureen   Oh, don't worry. Your Aunt Maureen'll take you on. Yes, I'm proud to say the Maureen Mauchline Agency is run by and for Scottish halfwits.

Barry   Why? Why? Why? Why? Why? Why?

Candice   What's up with him?

Maureen   Oh, I think he wanted to be the son Gerard never had.

Candice   I know your face from college. But who are you exactly?

Barry   Why? Why? Why? Why? Why? (*Snapping out of it.*) What?

Candice   I said: who the fuck are you?

Barry   Who the fuck am I?

Candice   Yes, who the fuck are you?

Barry   I'm young and innocent and just starting out on life's journey and I'm the greatest actor of my generation.

Candice   Oh no you're not. It's me. I'm the greatest actor of my generation. I won the gold medal.

Barry   Yes, but I was told I am by Ewan Carlyle. And he's the greatest actor of *his* generation.

Maureen   Oh you're all the greatest actors of your generation. You're the only type I'd have in the Maureen Mauchline Agency of Soho Square . . . Soho . . . London . . . Soho Square . . . Soho . . . London . . . Soho Square . . . Soho . . . London.

Maureen *goes out, chanting into the distance.*

Candice *and* **Barry** *go to follow, but* **Barry** *holds back.* **Candice** *turns back.*

Candice   You coming or not, prick?

Barry   I'll catch up with you.

Candice *goes.* **Barry** *goes over to cassette deck, puts in tape and presses play. It hisses. He stops it, takes it out and, turning it over, puts it back in. It still hisses.*

Barry Come on. Come on.

He presses fast forward, then presses play. It still hisses. **Dorothy** *comes in with cases, ready to go.*

Dorothy I told you to be gone by the time we got back.

Barry I'm going. I'm going. Don't you worry. Just as soon as /

Gerard *comes in with cases, ready to go. Beat.*

Barry *(steeling himself)* All right. All right. I'm going to say it. Sorry. I eh / I eh / (*To* **Gerard***, suddenly facing him.*) Why did you mentor me?

Gerard Oh well eh . . .

Barry Come on. Out with it.

Gerard Well I eh . . .

Barry Just tell me the truth. I can take it.

Gerard Out of the goodness of my heart possibly?

Barry *snorts.*

Gerard Because I like you perhaps?

Barry Hah!

Gerard All right. Maybe it was to give something back to theatre after all it's /

Barry You liar. You creep. You / You /

Suddenly the fax erupts into life, printing out. They all look round at it. Beat. **Dorothy** *goes to go over to it.* **Gerard** *stops her.*

Gerard Just leave it, Dorothy. It's time to go.

Dorothy . . . All right, Gerard. All right.

They pick up cases. Radio ad comes on. They all look round at the radio. **Gerard** *does nothing.*

Dorothy   What is that? (*To* **Barry**.) Was that you?

She goes to switch it off.

Barry (*blocking her way*)   You see! You see! You see! You see!

Barry *and* **Gerard** *stare each other out. Radio ad finishes and it becomes clear fax is pouring out paper.* **Dorothy** *rushes over to it.*

Gerard (*trying to block her, too late*)   Just leave it, Dorothy, I said!

Dorothy (*reading*)   I'll be more than . . . pleased to join your . . . new London agency. Alex Docherty. I'd love to, Maureen. Rachel Hart. I'm up for that. Can't wait. Dorothy does nothing for me anyway. Johnny Kelly. Tim says yes yes yes yes. Tim Goddard. Absolutely. Annie Merchant. (*Rushing through them.*) Jane Whyte. Billy Angelus. Lena McAvoy. Graeme Gilroy. Oh my God, Gerard. What are we going to do now?

Gerard   Nothing. We've retired. Come on.

Maureen *comes in.*

Maureen   Will you get a move on, Barry? Your Aunt Maureen didn't shell out 2K for you to be hanging about at the wrong end of Sauchiehall Street.

Dorothy   I hope you hate yourself for what you've done to me, Maureen Mauchline.

Maureen   Oh I do, Dorothy Darvel. I do. So thank God you taught me to love hating myself, eh? . . . But do you not love hating yourself for never giving Gerard the son he never had?

Dorothy   What are you talking about now, you halfwit?

Gerard   What's this?

Dorothy   Ignore her, Gerard.' She's doomed. The London vultures will have her for breakfast.

Gerard   No come on. Let's hear the girl. (*To* **Maureen**.) Maureen!

Maureen   Well the reason she didn't give you any children was /

Dorothy   No, Maureen. Please, no.

Gerard   Shut up, Dorothy.

Maureen   The reason was . . .

Dorothy   It's lies, Gerard. It's all lies, lies, nothing but lies.

Maureen   Well actually the reason she didn't give you the son you never had was / No, I'm sorry. I can't tell you, Gerard. Because an actors' agent never gives away secrets. Do they, Dorothy?

She grabs **Barry** *and takes him out. Pause.*

Gerard   What did I tell you? You give and give and give to the young cunt. Soon as he's got what he wants, it's offski. (*Shouting after* **Barry** *through street exit.*) But good on you, son. I'd have been exactly the same. You're an actor through and through. Selfish to the . . . (*To* **Dorothy**.) So have you got something to tell me?

Dorothy   No, dear. What would I have to say to you? . . . Have you got something to tell me?

Gerard   Well eh are you ready to go?

Dorothy (*referring to cassette*)   About that!

Gerard *shakes his head.*

Dorothy   Oh come off it, Gerard. I'd know that fruity hammy voice of yours anywhere!

Gerard   I was desperate. You know I owed money and / and /

Dorothy   Money?

Gerard   Yes. You know I did.

Dorothy   You mean you took money for that?

Gerard   Well why else would I prostitute my / ?

Dorothy I can't believe you took money for work and didn't offer me my commission.

Gerard It was a tiny amount, Dorothy. I /

Dorothy Don't you 'tiny amount' me. When I married you we agreed that all commissions were to be paid in full. No exceptions.

Gerard *takes out his wallet and gives* **Dorothy** *£20.*

Dorothy Thank you.

Gerard You're welcome . . . Are you ready now then?

Dorothy For what, dear?

Gerard For the cruise, Dorothy. We're late as it is.

Dorothy I beg your pardon, Gerard Galston. There won't be any cruise now. I've been up a close in Sauchiehall Street for thirty years establishing this business. And if it takes another thirty to re-establish it, then so be it. So be it. So bloody be it!

Gerard Oh Dorothy, Oh Dorothy, Oh Dorothy, Oh Dorothy.

Gerard *heads to exit.*

Dorothy And where do you think you're going?

Gerard Oh Dorothy. Oh Dorothy. Oh Dorothy. Oh Dorothy.

He goes out to street, chanting sotto voce. **Dorothy** *stands defiant as she is engulfed in paper from all directions.*

Slow fade.